بِسْمِ اللهِ الرَّحْمَنِ الرَّحِيمِ

1

Pinnacle Papers
VOLUME 5

الإِسْلامُ وَمُشْكِلاتُ الشَّبَابِ

Islam and the Problems of the Youth

By
Imam Muḥammad Saʿīd Ramaḍān al-Būṭī

Translated by
Mahdi Lock

NAWA BOOKS

We at Nawabooks would like to express our appreciation to everybody who contributed in making this book a reality. We pray that Allah ﷻ bestow His blessings upon it by guiding readers of this book closer towards Allah ﷻ and His beloved Prophet Muhammad ﷺ.

Pinnacle Papers: A Collection of Masterpieces by Imam Muḥammad Saʿīd Ramaḍān al-Būṭī

الإِسْلامُ وَمُشْكِلاتُ الشَّبَابِ

Islam and the Problems of the Youth

© Nawabooks, 2022

Originally Published by:	Dar Al Fikr 2020
Published by:	Nawabooks
Published in:	December 2022
Website:	www.nawabooks.com
Email:	nawabooks@gmail.com
Author:	Imam Muḥammad Saʿīd Ramaḍān al-Būṭī
Translated by:	Mahdi Lock

ISBN:	978-981-18-6016-4
Cover by:	Muhammadan Press

TABLE OF CONTENTS

ABOUT THE AUTHOR

 Imam Muḥammad Saʿīd Ramaḍan Al-Būṭī is one of the foremost Muslim theologians and legal scholars of this age. Born in 1929 in the village of Ayn Dewar in northern Syria, the imam moved to Damascus at the age of four with his father, the great scholar Mullā Ramaḍān al-Būṭī ﷺ, where he received his primary and secondary education. In 1953, he joined the Faculty of Sharīʿah at the University of al-Azhar in Cairo, Egypt, graduating with a first class in 1955. The following year he obtained a Diploma in Education from the Faculty of Arabic Language at the same University.

In 1958, the Imam was appointed as a teacher at the secondary school in Homs and in 1961, he was appointed as a lecturer in the Faculty of Sharīʿah at the University of Damascus. In 1965, at the University of al-Azhar once again, he obtained his doctorate with high distinction and a recommendation for a teaching post. That same year, he was appointed as a teacher in the Faculty of Sharīʿah at the University of Damascus, then an assistant professor and finally a full professor. He became the vice dean of that college in 1975 and then the dean in 1977. A few years later, he was appointed head of the department of Theology and Comparative Religion.

In addition to his lecturing, Imam al-Būṭī wrote around sixty books covering various Islamic sciences and subjects, the most prominent ones being *Fiqh al-Sīrah* (The Jurisprudence of the Prophetic Biography), *Kubrā al-Yaqīniyyāt al-Kawniyyah* (The Greatest Universal Sureties) and his four-volume commentary on the spiritual aphorisms of Imam Ibn ʿAṭāʾillāh al-Askandarī. He was also very active in teaching common believers in local masjids, especially Masjid al-Īmān in Damascus, and on television, recordings of which can be found online and especially on the site www.naseemalsham.com. He also served as the imam at the Umayyad Grand Masjid in Damascus for Friday prayers, a post he held for decades.

On March 21, 2013, Imam al-Būṭī, along with approximately fifty students, was murdered by terrorists while teaching Qurʾānic commentary in Masjid al-Īmān. Despite the immense trials and tribulations that Syria was and is still enduring, Imam al-Būṭī ﷺ was never dissuaded from his dedicated service to knowledge. After a funeral prayer that was attended by thousands of people, the Imam was buried next to Imam Ṣalāḥ al-Dīn al-Ayyūbī ﷺ in Bāb al-Saghīr graveyard in Damascus. May the Lord ﷻ bless and have mercy on him and all of us.

TRANSLATOR'S INTRODUCTION & ACKNOWLEDGEMENTS

All praise belongs to Allah, Lord of all creation, who forgives sins and with Him alone is every success. There is no power or strength except in Him. As Allah has honoured this miserable slave with the completion of such a task, all I ask is that He increase the blessings He has already bestowed upon me and to make me a better believer, cleanse my heart and grant me further strength to serve Him and the Ummah of His Beloved, ṣallā Allahu ʿalayhi wa sallam.

As for the creation, I begin by thanking Ustādh Muhammad Jalaluddeen of Nawa Books, once again, for taking on the beautiful project of translating and publishing the Pinnacle Papers into English, this book being the *fifth* volume in the series. Again, may Allah reward him immensely in this life and the next, protect him from harm, and grant him a long, healthy life full of worship and righteousness, āmīn!

I must also thank Dr Maḥmūd Ramaḍān for his constant support, yet again, and for always being on hand to answer questions. May Allah reward him, his father, his grandfather, and his entire family in abundance in this life and the next, āmīn!

Then there is proofreading. I ask Allah to reward my dear friend Hazem Mahdy who, as I have mentioned before, speaks both Arabic and English like a native. Again, he read both the Arabic text and the translation and made sure that everything was not only correct but also readable. We spent about a month reviewing several parts of the text, going back and forth and making sure that both of us were satisfied. May Allah reward him repeatedly in this life and in the Hereafter, āmīn! Ustādh Jalaluddeen, as he always does, also read over the text and pointed out a couple of things. As always, I must stress, however, that any errors or shortcomings that still remain are solely my responsibility. We praise Allah the Exalted for any benefit that comes out of this work. Only the mistakes are mine.

Lastly, I thank my wife for her patience, serenity and encouragement throughout the translation process. May Allah reward her and her parents immensely, āmīn!

When I first came across this book, I was expecting to see Imam al-Būṭī advise the youth exclusively and that he would do so, as I have seen in all of his other books that I have translated, in a way that is unique and powerful. What I saw upon reading the book was far beyond my expectations. For years, I had heard Muslims, in both the East and the West, talk about "the youth" and the problems and difficulties they encounter, and every discussion was confined to advising the youth. No discussion, to my knowledge, took a step back and looked at the bigger picture. This is what Imam al-Būṭī has done; "the youth" are not a group of people existing in a vacuum. Instead, they are a reflection and indication of the general state of their community, or society. If that community is healthy and sound, that health will be reflected in the youth. Likewise, if that community is diseased, that disease will be visible in the youth. Therefore, the "problems of the youth" are not the problems of the youth per se but actually the problems of the entire community.

The imam also articulated, in brilliant fashion, something that I had noticed while living in Muslim countries but could not put into words, which is the mixed messaging that the youth are given by their elders and the wider community they inhabit. On the one hand, they are told that they are Muslims and that Islam is the One True Religion. On the other, they are told that they should imitate the Americans, the British, or the French in their ways and customs. At school, they are advised to read works by Muslim scholars but are also told to read works by unbelievers as if they are of equal value, books that contradict what those Muslim scholars say. All of this, of course, leads to contradiction and cognitive dissonance. If young people in the Muslim world seem confused and befuddled, this is why.

But enough about teachers or the community at large. The first guardians of the youth are the parents, which means that this book is actually advice to the parents, especially the conclusion. If you are a parent, you should want, more than anything, a righteous child. It is that child who will make *du'ā'* for you when you have left this world and recite the Qur'ān on your behalf. It is that child who will intercede for you, if it is indeed necessary, when you stand before Allah. Furthermore, you want that righteous child to love you and respect you. You earn his respect by practising what you preach. If you stress to him that he is a Muslim and that he must follow Islam's rulings, he will expect to see Islam in you. If he does not, he will see a contradiction. If your life is a contradiction, your children's lives will also be a contradiction, and they might seek certainty somewhere else.

This is the core of what the Imam is telling us. We need to get our homes in order, first and foremost. Our homes need to be abodes of worship and obedience to our Lord.

And with Allah alone is every success.

ABOUT THE TRANSLATOR

Mahdi Lock is a professional freelance translator of classical Arabic Islamic texts into English. He has a BA in Arabic and History from the University of Leeds, an MA in Arabic Linguistics from King Abdul Aziz University in Jeddah, and a Diploma in Translation from the Chartered Institute of Linguists in London, of which he is also a Member (MCIL). He has been studying theology, law and other Islamic sciences for several years with teachers in England, North Africa and the Middle East. To date, his translated works include *Kitāb al-Ḥalāl wa al-Ḥarām* by Imam Abū Ḥāmid al-Ghazālī, *Kitāb al-Waqf* from *al-Mughnī al-Muḥtāj* by al-Khaṭīb al-Shirbīnī, the introduction to *al-Majmūʿ* by Imam Yaḥyā al-Nawawī and *Sharḥ al-Ṣudūr* by Imam Jalāl al-Dīn al-Suyūṭī.

FOREWORD - ARABIC

بسم الله الرحمن الرحيم

الحمد لله رب العالمين، والصلاة والسلام على سيدنا محمد المبعوث رحمة للعالمين

وعلى آله وصحبه ومن تبعهم بإحسان إلى يوم الدين وبعد

الشباب هم الطاقة المتوثبة التي بها تنهض الأمم ... هم الطاقة المنتجة ... هم

حصن الأمة وعنوان قوتها... هم أمل الأمة لغدها المشرق.

أولى النبي ﷺ الشباب اهتمامه، فكانوا مادة الإسلام والعنصر الفاعل في كل

مراحل الدعوة في العصر النبوي. وفي مقدمتهم سيدنا علي ﷺ. ومنهم عبد الله بن

عمر وعبد الله بن عباس وعبد الله بن الزبير، وأسامة بن زيد، وزيد بن ثابت كاتب

الوحي وجامع القرآن والمشرف على نسخه.

ولذلك فقد استهدفهم أعداء الإسلام، وخططوا لإجهاض هذه الطاقة من

خلال إثارة غرائزهم، وتبديد اهتماماتهم، واستهدفوا فكرياً لتشكيكهم بدينهم، بعد أن

تمكنوا من إبعادهم عن المعارف الدينية الصحيحة إلى حد بعيد، أضف إلى ذلك أن

العدو بذل وسعه ليضعف بناء الأسرة مما جعلهم يعانون من تناقضات في علاقتهم مع

الأبوين، وعلاقتهم مع الجهات التي تريد أن تفرض وصايتها على تفكيرهم وسلوكهم.

ضللوا الشباب باسم العلم فأغرقوهم في نظريات وفرضيات سميت علماً، بينما هي بعيدة عن المنهج العلمي الصحيح. فمن داروينية إلى جدلية ديالكتيكية إلى فرويدية ... مما لا يستند إلى قاعدة علمية معتبرة. وجعلوا تلك الترهات التي سموها علماً بديلاً عن الحقائق العلمية التي تبصرهم بالمعرفة الصحيحة، بالدليل العلمي الذي يعرفهم على الكون والإنسان والحياة ... ويوضح لهم وظيفة الإنسان في هذا الكون.

ليس للشباب مشكلة سوى أنهم ضحية تضليل استهدفهم ليعانوا من الضياع النفسي والضلال العقلي والانحراف السلوكي. بينما هم الطاقة الفاعلة والمنتجة والمبدعة، مما جعلهم طاقة مبددة وعبئاً على المجتمع.

وهذا الكتّاب يعالج ما يعاني منه الشباب من ضياع يستهدف تبديد طاقاتهم البناءة وعقولهم المبدعة وفطرتهم الصافية الطاهرة. ليبقى المجتمع في حالة تفكك وضياع.

إنني لأشكر الأستاذ مهدي لوك على ترجمة هذا الكتّاب، وآمل أن يكون علاجاً لكثير من الشباب الضائعين، ليجدوا فيه دليلاً إلى سعادتهم وهدايتهم. كما أشكر الدار الناشرة وأرجو أن ينال الجميع حظه من الثواب والأجر من الله تعالى.

والحمد لله رب العالمين

محمد توفيق رمضان البوطي

FOREWORD - ENGLISH

In the Name of Allah, the All Merciful, the Most Merciful

All praise be to Allah, Lord of all Creation, and blessings and peace be upon our master Muḥammad, the one sent as a mercy to all of creation, and upon his Family, his Companions, and those who have followed them in excellence until the Day of Repayment.

To proceed:
Young people are the awakening force with which nations rise... They are the productive force... They are the fortress of the nation and the sign of its strength... They are the nation's hope for a bright tomorrow.

The Prophet ﷺ paid special attention to the youth; they were the fundamental component of Islam and its active element in all stages of calling people to Islam in the Prophet's era. At the forefront of them is our master Ali ؓ, followed by ʿAbdullah ibn ʿUmar, ʿAbdullah ibn ʿAbbās, ʿAbdullah ibn az-Zubayr, Usāmah ibn Zayd, and Zayd bin Thabit, the one who wrote down the Revelation, who collected the Qurʾān, and the one who was in charge of its copies.

This is why the enemies of Islam have targeted the youth, and have plotted to abort this energy by stirring up their natural impulses and dissipating their genuine interests. They have targeted them intellectually by raising doubts about their Religion, and they do this after having managed to distance them from sound religious knowledge to a large extent. Furthermore, the enemy has deployed all of its assets towards weakening the family structure so that they suffer from contradictions in their relationships with their parents as well as in their relationships with those who want to impose their tutelage on how they think and behave.

They have misled the youth in the name of "science", and have then drowned them in theories and hypotheses that have been called "science", while, in fact, they are all far removed from the correct scientific method. From Darwinism to dialectical materialism to Freudianism ... none of which is based on any significant scientific base. They have made these fairy tales that they have called "science" a substitute for the scientific facts, which can enlighten the youth with sound knowledge, based on scientific evidence that informs them about the universe, man and life... and explains to them man's role in this universe.

Young people have no problem other than that they are victims of deception that is targeted at them in order to make them suffer psychological damage, mental delusion, and behavioural deviation, while, in actual fact, they are our active, productive and creative force. They have been made a spent force and a burden on society.

This book discusses the damage suffered by young people, damage that is aimed at dissipating their productive capacities, creative minds and their pure nature, so that the community can remain in a state of disintegration and ruin.

I thank Ustādh Mahdi Lock for translating this book, and I hope that it will be a cure for many lost youth, and that it thus shows them the way towards happiness and guidance. I also thank the publishing house, and I hope that everyone will receive his share of reward for Allah the Exalted. And all praise be to Allah, Lord of all Creation.

Muḥammad Tawfīq Ramaḍān al-Būṭī

INTRODUCTION TO THE SECOND EDITION

Regarding the second edition of this book, I have nothing to say other than that I praise Allah 🐝 for making most of the youth of our aware generation able to sense their problems, to be concerned about them, and to strive to find a sound solution to them.

Maybe many of our youth suffer from some of the problems that I spoke about in this book, and maybe many of them are helpless when faced with them. The vast majority of them, however, reluctantly submit to them, wandering aimlessly in their vortex. They are waiting for someone to help them, whom they can cling on to, and they are looking out for someone to guide them and show them.

I realised this when four thousand copies of this book were sold within four weeks, and from the nature of the groups and organisations that turned to it and devoted themselves to it!

If someone who has a problem realises that he is suffering from a problem, he is halfway towards solving it, and how easy is it to complete the second half when the way is clearly delineated, and the light of truth is clearly visible.

Who, then, remains?

There remains a tiny minority of youth who flounder in their problems, without sensing that they are problems. In fact, they do not like it when someone comes and tries to make them aware of them, and warn them about their consequences, and thus we will overlook them and the situation they are in. The only thing awaiting them is the trials and tribulations of time, and that will happen to them soon enough.

I present the second edition of this book to anyone who has a desire to know the truth, regardless of his conduct and regardless of what is in his mind and thoughts. I only ask him to nourish this desire of his with more study and research, and to remove himself further from his own inclinations and prejudices.

When he has become aware of the problems that I am talking about, and believes in the remedies that I am proposing, all I hope from him is that he spare no energy in implementing those remedies, and not just in matters that concern him as an individual but that which concerns the community as a whole.

I can only write and speak, and I am not sparing any energy in that regard. However, those besides me have other means of remedy at their disposal, so let us be consumed by solicitude for the truth, which we believe in. Then, let us combine our means of remedy and implementation, and let us join our efforts in this cause.

By Allah, this is the smallest levy that humanity imposes on man.

Damascus, Ṣafar, 1393 AH

Muḥammad Saʿīd Ramaḍān al-Būṭī

INTRODUCTION TO THE FIRST EDITION

I was thinking about presenting this topic as a lecture to young people; I would not communicate it to them – as I am now – by way of writing something down or publishing a book. Rather, I would discuss it with them directly. I would then confer with them and let them express any opinions they might have, or maybe raise hidden problems that they have noticed and which I have not.

However, it is Allah's predestination that decides! It was not facilitated for me to meet with young people, and thus I was not given the opportunity to present what I had to them and hear what they have to say. Then I found myself sitting in my office trying to compensate for all of the above by writing…and I was seeking refuge and assistance from the pen, that sublime, divine gift that helps me elucidate what my tongue is aware of, and allows me to connect with my brethren when there are no means to meet in person.

I ask Allah to perpetuate this gift that He has bestowed upon me, that it remain an open window through which the contents of my heart penetrate peoples' souls, and from which others can be shown signs to every truth and goodness.

To talk about the problems of the youth is to talk about the axis of all social problems. Treating all the various social ailments can only start from a primary, foundational point, which is to treat the circumstances and problems of the youth. There cannot be sound growth in a community if the youth are not removed from the various forms of evil and deviation.

This is why, when an enemy wants to corrupt and ruin a nation, it focuses its efforts on corrupting and ruining its youth. Likewise, the most important pillars of civilisation cannot be established unless they are based on nurturing the youth, both intellectually and psychologically.

What is the Ummah as a whole? It is children preparing themselves to become youth, youth chasing their hopes and ambitions in this life and expending their energy and vitality while doing so, and elderly people savouring the echoes of their youth and living on what remains of its goodness and energy.

Life, therefore, is nothing more than striving towards the phase of youth, or enjoying the goodness of youth and its pleasures, or relying on the beautiful memories of youth and what remains of its blessings.

In a person's life, youth is a collection of aspiring energies. If they are directed towards uprightness and goodness, the entire Ummah will see immense benefit from these energies. If they are directed towards deviation and injustice, the entire Ummah will suffer calamitous consequences.

This is why the Messenger of Allah ﷺ made it clear that the young person who grows up properly, in obedience to Allah the Exalted, is right behind the just ruler in terms of reward. As for the remaining five of the seven categories that the Messenger of Allah ﷺ enumerated, and whom Allah will shade with the shade of His throne on the Day when there is no shade but His,[1] all of them, despite their precedence and immense rank with Allah ﷻ, are not as high as the first two!

---

1 The two Shaykhs have related this ḥadīth.

The ḥadīth shows that the young person who grows up worshipping Allah has a positive and rectifying effect on his community that is almost equivalent to the ruler's capacity for rectification; the former does it with his inherent capacities and energies while the latter does so with his acquired mandatory power.

There is no doubt that the opposite is also true. The young person who is deviant in his conduct will have a harmful effect on his community that is almost equivalent to the evil effect that a tyrannical or deviant ruler has.

Therefore, to talk about the problems of the youth, and to analyse them and look at ways to remedy them, is a study of the utmost importance and gravity. They must be looked at and treated scientifically and sincerely.

From where, then, do the problems of the youth arise? What are the nature of these problems and their types? And how can they be dealt with and eliminated?

Those are the foundations of this treatise. I ask Allah the Most High, the All-Powerful, to grant me success in treating them, and that with my reading brethren I arrive at radical solutions to these problems, solutions that go beyond the bounds of my writing and others' reading.

I say this while imagining that my discussion of this topic might come to no avail (and I hope to Allah that I am wrong in this imagination).

The reason is that those who lose sleep at night because of the problems of the youth and confer about their causes and treatment do not have any treatment, let alone the means to implement it. All they can do is elucidate them, warn against them, and point out how they might be treated. **None of that will ever lead to treatment and rectification on its own.**

For how long have conferences been held to address this problem, books and studies published, and different theories and opinions presented without our finding any fruit or benefit in terms of implementation. In fact, the upcoming generation has continued to suffer from its problems and the community has continued to suffer as a result.

The conferences and publications have turned out to be words just like any other words. They cannot miraculously change or rectify anything.

Again, however, I ask Allah the Exalted that I be mistaken in what I imagine, and that He grant these words that I am about to write a spirit of influence and implementation.

And whatever the result may be, we shall treat this issue while obeying Allah the Exalted's words:

$$﴿ قَالُواْ مَعْذِرَةً إِلَىٰ رَبِّكُمْ وَلَعَلَّهُمْ يَتَّقُونَ ﴾$$

"They said: 'So that we have an excuse to present to your Lord, and so that maybe they will have taqwā.'" [al-'A'rāf 7:164][2]

---

2 (tn): the full verse, and the one that follows, is: **"When a group of them said: 'Why do you rebuke a people whom Allah is going to destroy or severely punish?' they said: 'So that we have an excuse to present to your Lord, and so that maybe they will have taqwā.'** Then when they forgot what they had been reminded of, We rescued those who had forbidden the evil and seized those who did wrong with a harsh punishment because they were deviators." [al-'A'rāf 7:164-5]

And my reliance is upon Allah, and He is in charge of guidance and success.

Rajab, 1393 AH

Muḥammad Saʿīd Ramaḍān al-Būṭī

From Where Do the Problems of the Youth Arise?

Before everything else, we start by asking: are the youth actually suffering from a problem?

The truth is that the youth (as such), wherever they may be, do not have any problem. That is, they do not quarrel with themselves or their intellects, over anything, anywhere or at any time, as long as they are intelligent and submit to the authority of mankind and his natural law.

They did, and they still do, conduct themselves in their intellectual and psychological affairs in a way that is harmonious with the exigencies of human nature and man's rational and intellectual proclivities.

They might err or stray, but that is not because of a problem that is exclusive to them because they are youth. Rather, they will share in that problem with other groups of people, and they will be driven therein by some common denominator, such as factors of tribalism,[3] psychological responses, or complying with traditions and customs.

Therefore, where did this huge title come from, which has reached the point of becoming a global issue? It has reached the point that talking about **the problems of the youth** is to talk about a serious scientific matter; all the media are talking about it and trying to treat it, along with all the magazines in the world and a great number of periodicals, books, and treatises.

---

3 Ar. *'aṣabiyyah*, which could also be translated as misguided enthusiasm.

This title has been a superficial personification of a malady that has manifested itself in the youth and no one else.

Superficial people have supposed that the element of the youth is the source and cause of this malady, and that some anomaly has infiltrated the psychological or intellectual makeup of these youth! They thus proceeded to research, to treat, and to give various prescriptions for *individuals* among the youth, and to turn the attention of scholars and educators towards their awful state and the need to work towards correcting it.

However, they have, without doubt, researched to no avail, and their treatments have not produced any cure, because it is not the youth who are ill. Rather, they are merely reflecting the state of someone else who is ill! **So, who is actually ill?**

It is the community that they are living in! Any problem that manifests itself in their behaviour and in their lives is nothing but an effect of the community's illness.

The one who looks at what is called 'the problems of the youth' and then confines his attention and his contemplation to their affairs and their proclivities while claiming that he is trying to treat them and nurture them is like someone who takes his car down a bumpy road that is full of rocks and potholes and when he sees his car shaking and vibrating and not being able to move in a straight line, he gets out and then spends hours staring at its engine and other internal parts trying to figure out what could be wrong!

In the minds and souls of the youth, wherever they may be, there is no illness or bane that they are suffering from. Rather, they are like a sensor that displays everything that is concealed in the community: the chaos, the confusion, and the disorder.

If the middle-aged and the elderly enjoyed the same sensitivity that the youth do, they would suffer the same problems that they do.

In order to make this matter clearer, you should know that a person only enters the battlefield of life armed with his intellectual and psychological capacities.

However, neither of them develops during his initial stage – when it is nothing more than a divine gift that has come from the unseen – beyond being like the small seed of a lofty tree. It is only with time that these intellectual and psychological seeds will turn into fruit-bearing trees with various branches. In other words, it is over a long period of time that a person gains experiences that nurture and develop his different emotions and sentiments.

Some of these experiences and these skills are planned and intended, and they are what educational scholars call the factors of "deliberate education", such as school and the like. The rest – and they are the majority – are involuntary and are not planned or directed, such as environment, genes, and so forth.

Therefore, the intellectual and psychological personality of a young person is mostly influenced by the community, by way of both direct and indirect factors.

The young person, therefore, is undoubtedly the most accurate reflection of the community that he is in; if it is good, he is good, and if it is bad, he is bad.

And whatever manifestations of good or bad that we see in this reflection are nothing more than an illustration of the state of the community, whether it is sound or it is corrupt.

You might ask: but what is the difference?

Why is the state of the community not a depiction of the healthy or corrupt state of the nation's youth, rather than the other way around?

You can find the answer in what has been stated above. It has been made clear to you, in what we have mentioned, that it is the young person who receives his nurturing and education, whether directly or indirectly, from the community. It is not the community that is formed by a single youth.

And what is the community? It is the house, the school, the street, the masjid, the place of entertainment, the shop, the factory, the office, inasmuch as all of that is surrounded by concepts, values, and ideas.

There is no doubt that the guiding force in all of these facilities and amenities is the collective influence of individuals, laws, and the ideas of scholars and influential personalities, which have their pedagogical and nurturing authority over individuals and especially over the youth.

However, this interaction between the influenced and influencer continues and does not stop.

The individuals and scholars who influence the community are only carrying out a trust that was granted to them by the previous community, in that it had authority and influence over them.

This is how it is: the community in any age is influenced by the one that preceded it and it influences the one that comes after it.

After what we have mentioned, maybe you will ask the following:

Are the researchers who stay up at night thinking about how to treat "the problem of the youth" not aware of this fact, which everyone should know?

Why do they focus their attention on that which reflects the effects of the problem and not look at the community, which is the source and foundation of the problem?[4]

The answer is that they know this fact, or most of them do, yet despite that, they do not look at the community, which is where the illness hides and is the source of the problem. This is because they are happy with the community the way it is. Despite its ills and evils, it suits their desires and pleasures.

Thus, they and the community are like an alcoholic and wine; he is aware of its harms and he can see the horrible effects it has on his body, but, despite that, he is addicted to it. He tries to rid his body of this filth by using sedative medicines and therapies, which do not benefit him at all.

The disease is in the community, and the researchers most certainly know this, but they cannot renounce its delightful malady, just like an alcoholic cannot put down his glass of aged wine.

However, they find themselves face to face with the harmful and burdensome effects of this malady, embodied in what they call "the problems of the youth". Thus, their discomfort and dissatisfaction with these problems pushes them towards a useless type of resistance against them. It is like someone who has spilled sweets all over his clothes and body and flies are gathering all around him and all he does is brush them away with his hands every time they annoy him or disturb him.

---

4 Most western researchers, as well as the easterners who ride their coattails, think that the problem of the youth is a pathological phenomenon whose roots are concealed within young people themselves, and for reasons that are connected to them personally.

This person continues to incline towards making gains without suffering any losses, towards earning and not losing.

He trusts the social situation that he is in, because it titillates his dreams and responds to his desires and passions, yet, despite that, he is dissatisfied with their results and effects. He then strives in vain to resist divine wisdom, and to cut off these results from their causes, so that maybe he can enjoy the causes and not have to worry about the burdensome consequences.

This is man's biggest problem in this life.

We should now examine the categories of these problems and how important they are, **taking into consideration our small Islamic community.**

This is because we have nothing to do with those other, remote communities that we have no sway over.

At the end of our research, we will find that our discussion about the problems of the youth falls back, in large part, on imitating the West in everything that it brings and leaves behind.

Otherwise, the problems of the youth for us would not even be a small portion of the same problems that people have to deal with in the West.

However, whatever the case may be, we are going down a path, and our community is being pushed, by the deaf and the dumb, to imitate western communities. The more we draw nearer to them, the more of their problems we come to suffer.

Let us thus treat them with a prescription and with words, and maybe Allah will allow for someone to treat them with action and application. We will now talk about the categories of these problems.

The Problems of Education[5] and Knowledge[6]

There is nothing more beloved to the educated young person today than to know. In other words, he loves to behold something unknown and then subject it to all the means of knowledge and information that he has at his disposal, starting with books of knowledge and moving on to newspapers, magazines, lectures, conferences, television, radio, and even the cinema and the street!

If the community busied themselves with this desire of the youth and mobilised all the means of knowledge and information available to them to serve this reality, unveil its secrets, and arrive at sound knowledge, out of these youth would arise a huge multitude of insightful scholars who would study a great deal of the realities of this universe.

But the community has not taken advantage of this desire, and most of these youth have not benefitted at all from their educational undertakings and quests for knowledge.

One of these young people will dedicate himself to studying something and in the end – by his own admission – he has nothing to show for it.

---

5 Ar. *ath-thaqāfah*, which can be translated as 'culture' or 'education'. Please see the footnote below.
6 Ar. *al-'ilm*, which refers to both knowledge *and* science.

One of them will be drawn to the study of philosophy and its theories, hoping that it will lead him to true knowledge and the secrets of the universe. At the end of his journey, however, he has more ignorance, has graver doubts, and is more confused.

Another person will try to equip himself with a portion of his nation's culture[7] in the hope that it will help him find solutions to the difficulties that he has taken on, but he finds himself taking on more baffling social problems and difficulties!

This is an illustration of the problem.

What, however, are its essential roots and factors?

The answer is that the word *'ilm*, which used to be the most accurate word in terms of meaning and definition, no longer has a defined meaning in our community.

Instead, it has become one of those high-sounding words that accommodate several meanings!

In logic, *'ilm* means **to understand something as it truly is in reality**. An understanding is not called *'ilm* unless there are sufficient proofs that such an understanding corresponds with reality and the facts. At that point, it does not matter whether the issue is something natural and therefore subject to experience and observation, or something abstract, and therefore subject to contemplation and reflection.

---

7 Ar. *ath-thaqāfah*, which is the knowledges of the lives of nations, their history, their customs, and their ideas, and thus, every nation has a *thaqāfah* that distinguishes it. It seems that there is no exception to this generalisation apart from the Arab nation, whose *thaqāfah* is piece and parts of the *thaqāfah* of others.

One of the most obvious consequences of this is that the word *'ilm* can never apply to two different understandings of one reality. One of the two must contradict the facts of the matter and therefore cannot be *'ilm*.

However, today this word – according to its prevalent meaning – is applied to an unlimited number of theories, opinions, and ideas connected to all kinds of things, regardless of whether they differ with or contradict one another!

Now, any intellectual treatment of some reality is worthy of granting a conclusion that could end up being called *'ilm*, bearing all the sanctity, inviolability, and esteem that this word does, provided that one condition is met, which is that this treatment be branded **scientific research.**[8]

Research is deemed "scientific" for no reason other than that the researcher follows a specific method that rises above religious beliefs and related matters of the unseen. Based on this condition alone, it is possible for "scientific research" to arrive at definitive, scientific laws while at the same time the researchers become "scientists". Then, anyone who sees himself as "scientific" in his thinking and certainty adopts their "science".

The undisputable conclusion is that these "scientific researches" arrive at scientific laws that are contradictory, even though they are connected to the same reality. Furthermore, despite this, the researchers are still called scientists of that one reality, even though they differ and may have numerous opinions regarding one scientific matter.

Let us present some examples.

---

8   Ar. *al-baḥth al-'ilmī*.

The educated young person turns to Islam in order to listen to its creed and its rulings, regarding the universe, man, and life. Then an afflatus from the community infiltrates his mind and says: 'You are a man of science. Religion is just beliefs in the unseen that have no basis. Instead, you should listen to what science says on the tongues of its leading figures. Listen to Kant, Descartes, Freud, Karl Marx, Darwin, Stuart Mill...'

Therefore, true knowledge about the universe, man, and life can only be found with these people, because they follow the scientific method and do not shackle themselves to beliefs in the unseen.

The young person listens to these people and scrutinises what each one of them says, and finds that the scientific conclusions of these scientists are contradictory and incongruent:

Descartes and Kant do not believe in Darwin's theory of evolution. Darwin does not agree with what Freud says about sex and its power over the ego. Those among them who view that the structure of the universe is based on the law of mechanics do not believe, as Marx and his followers do, that it is based on a dialectical structure.

And this is how each one of these researchers has his own school of thought that explains the universe and life. In many cases, their positions are so different from one another that they are complete opposites.

The educated young person who is called on by his community to study these individuals, on the basis that they are scientists and that their opinions regarding the universe and its secrets are science; which of the differing opinions does he rely on? Which one should he adopt and believe in?

Or is it the case that all of these differing, contradictory opinions are considered science and considered correct as long as they are the result of a method that is far removed from religion and what religion requires? In other words, is it the case that their scientific value is concealed in the fact they are devoid of the authority of religion, and not in the extent to which they are close to or indeed touching the truth itself?

This is where the problem starts. When he has this feeling, or this question in his mind, regardless of how tiny or hidden it might be, the first scientific or intellectual knot appears in the young person's soul. Then he might choose one of these contradictory "scientific" schools of thought, for some motive, be it social, psychological, educational, or utilitarian.

However, this school of thought that he embraces or adopts does not give him the same psychical contentment and tranquillity, or intellectual satisfaction, that a true, proper, scientific understanding does.

This is because when he adheres to one of these opinions, he only does so in order to adorn himself with a progressive idea in front of his peers and his community, or because he hopes some good will come of it, or to protect himself from some evil that is lurking. As for what is in the depths of his soul, and when he is all alone with his intellect, he oscillates between theories and hypotheses that have no beginning and no end. He will listen to a little bit of existentialist philosophy and then become aware of a Marxist refutation of that philosophy. He will scrutinise another school of thought to a minimal extent and then find refutations being flung at it from all sides.

He will flee from the crush and din of this debate in favour of the latest progressive idea about the universe that has been adopted by a large group of those who like to think of themselves as advocates of scientific research. That latest idea is what Darwin called to regarding life and the origin of species. However, once he has sat down to take a good look at this idea, it will not be long before he comes across

Neo-Darwinism,[9] which savagely attacks and attempts to destroy what the original Darwinism built. Once this attack has caught his attention, it will not be long before he becomes aware of another version of Darwinism that will be making every effort to demolish the previous two while presenting itself as a wholly new idea.

In the ocean of these impassioned "scientific" opinions that are in conflict with one another, the young person's psyche and mind are afflicted by a vortex of burdensome ignorance and painful confusion. He leaves his intellectual isolation **with an ego that rejects everything but also asks about everything**.

However, despite this, this feeling stays firmly within the depths of his soul, because there is no doubt that he exits his intellectual isolation and presents himself to people as calm and composed, carrying on as normal and continuing to defend the school of thought that he is associated with, for the reasons that we mentioned above.

When his display of intellectual firmness and his defence of what he is supposedly certain of are nothing more than a veil that covers the confusion and anxiety that pervade his soul, the confusion and anxiety only increase and grow. This person does not stop ruminating his doubts and concerns regarding everything, whenever he finds himself alone with his thoughts.

Despite the gravity of this problem, no one apart from the one suffering it is aware of it at this stage, because the problem lives, as we have said, deep inside his conscience and his delicate feelings.

It is not long, however, before this problem comes to be reflected in his conduct and in his relationships with others. **He will start to**

---

9   "Neo-Darwinism" refers to the theory that was proposed by the Dutch scientist Hugo de Vries in order to explain evolution, which was based on the hypothesis of mutation as opposed to Darwin's hypothesis of natural selection and survival of the fittest. See the book *'Ilm al-Ḥayāt al-Ḥayawāniyyah* by Dr 'Abdul Ḥalīm Suwaydān.

have contempt for everything, he will not set any life goals for himself, and he will not aspire to uphold any principle. Today, there are many young people like this in our community, and there is no doubt that their numbers are increasing.

Maybe one of these people will look for something to deliver him from these doubts and contradictions, and thus he will seek refuge in philosophy, thinking that because of the pomp and splendour of this word, its leading figures must have certain knowledge of everything.

As they used to say in the past, if you study only half of philosophy you will find yourself more ignorant and more confused. If you study all of it and plunge its depths, it will give you ample knowledge and a correct understanding of the realities of many things.

Most contemporary philosophers, who have spent their lives studying this field, have only travelled a quarter of the path, and thus their studying has given them a false view of things, and has implanted in them misgivings about everything.

These philosophers have written books and research papers, but they fill them with their intellectual misgivings more than they fill them with scientific facts.

And this is what the well-known masters do, the ones with big names and widespread fame, so what about those who imitate them and follow their footsteps, and write the way they do in order to adorn themselves and talk pompously?

Many of our youth today are infatuated with studying these individuals, reading their books, and being interested in their research. Their motive for doing so is what I have told you: among these great names they are looking for something that will save them from the doubts and contradictions of "scientists" regarding man, the universe, and life.

This studying, however, throws them into greater ignorance and deeper layers of darkness. Maybe they will come back doubting the value of the intellect itself, as I have noticed in a group of people.

Some time ago, a group of these youths visited me, and they had long hair and weird clothes. They started putting forward their questions about life and man, his origin and his final destination, so I asked them about the books they had studied and the schools of thought that they had arrived at. They enumerated a list of philosophical books that had been translated and told me that they had not benefitted from them at all. Instead, they ended up right back at the confusion that they had started with.

I said to them: The one who is lacking something cannot give it. These people, whose books you have read and whose ideas you have studied, are themselves in the greatest need of someone to save them from their confusion. All they do is examine philosophical schools, ancient and modern, and follow all of them while also critiquing them as they see fit.

It is futile to expect them to have a decisive opinion on something, because their position is nothing more than that of someone who examines and compares, and then is generally sceptical of all of it.

In the end, I said to them: scientific research in our age is a huge problem, and the first step towards solving it is that we learn how to read, and where to start reading.[10]

---

10 If Allah so wills, I shall expand on this when discussing solutions to these problems.

Furthermore, *thaqāfah* has its own role in aggravating the problem and making it worse.

Before anything else, we must be aware of the difference between *ʿilm* and *thaqāfah*.

ʿIlm is what we have said: to understand something as it truly is in reality and supported by proof, regardless of time or place.

As for *thaqāfah*, it is the knowledges and experiences that are connected to the nature of a nation, its heritage, its traditions, its community, and its pedagogical and behavioural conventions.

Nevertheless, it is *ʿilm* that is the commodity that can be exported and imported throughout the entire world. It should not be connected to a religion, principle, benefit, or tradition.

As for *thaqāfah*, despite the fact that it espouses scientific facts in many aspects, in its totality it is still considered part of the particular characteristics of a people or nation, woven according to its size[11] and applied to its life.

The educated and cultured[12] young person, therefore, is the one whose mind has blossomed in the nature of the environment that he is in, along with everything that it espouses: history, cultural norms, values, and conventions of pedagogy and behaviour.

---

11 (tn): i.e. each nation's culture is like a garment that fits it.
12 Ar. *muthaqqaf*.

Our community today, however, barely has a *thaqāfah*. It is similar to a bag that has been emptied of its original contents and then filled – like a vacuum – with incompatible parts of the cultures[13] of other nations.

When the young person turns his attention to the community in order to learn and equip himself from its *thaqāfah*, he falls into – because of what we mentioned – contradictions concerning the affairs of life, confusion regarding manners of pedagogy and behaviour, and incompatibility in how the community is structured and organised.

For example, we say that the understanding that is now espoused by the lifestyle of the "progressive" woman – in terms of her appearance, her working, and her mixing with men – does not agree with our economic reality, nor does it agree with our understanding of the structure of the family, in that the husband is the one responsible for the dowry and maintenance and he is the one in charge of the house and its affairs.

The pedagogical principles that the child adopts in our schools and hold sway over many of our homes do not agree with the nature of the values and principles that we, and our children, adhere to.

These pedagogical principles are imported from communities in which religion only applies to the nurturing of feelings and emotions. Meanwhile, for us, religion is rooted in the intellect and rational conviction. Emotion only has an auxiliary role.

This incompatibility between aspects of the *thaqāfah* that is prevalent in our community reflects, in the end, a dangerous type of incongruity in the psyche of the young people who imbibe this incompatible, mixed up *thaqāfah*.

---

13 Ar. *thaqāfāt*, the plural of *thaqāfah*.

Some of them will look at their glorious history, in the period of the Middle Ages, with the same eye of derision and scorn that Westerners look at this period of their history.

Some of them will refuse to do anything but subject their Islam, which has never known to have any enmity with or contradict any scientific fact, to the same melting-pot of "reformism" that Christianity was subjected to so that it could conform to the progress of ideas and science.

The Arabic language – which used to hold the treasure of a diverse *thaqāfah* – has now lost most of this treasure. After being emptied of its sublime literary contents, it has turned into a vessel that is overflowing with literary schools of thought and trends that are foreign and have nothing whatsoever to do with this language and its nature. The ears of the youth turn to these foreign schools and innovations and, in the end, turn away from studying their language and its nature along with the values, rules, and studies that it espouses.

These incompatible pieces of *thaqāfah*, whose parts are taken from here and there, do not bring about disastrous consequences for the community alone, in that it is a structured organisation that people live in. Rather, before any of that, they put confusion into the souls of the youth, who are the first to be afflicted by their maladies and the first to suffer from their contradictions.

One of the most significant effects of this confusion is that it eliminates the possibility of there being a clear vision of the facts and principles of Islam. It places between them and the young person thick barriers of ignorance that were never there to begin with.

The Problem of the Psychological Struggle

I reiterate what I told you before: these problems are not an illness that is concealed within the essence and souls of the youth. Rather, they are an illness that the community suffers from, and the problem of the youth is nothing more than a symptom of that same illness.

Therefore, what we call the psychological struggle among the youth is not some abnormality that suddenly appeared and they started feeling it. Rather, it is a reflection of something worse that has permeated the community in all of its aspects and institutions. It was inevitable that this would be clearly and gravely reflected in the psyche of the youth, which is the most accurate sensor of its kind. Thus, from which of the social maladies did the psychological struggle among the youth emerge?

The truth is that there are many, diverse maladies, but it is possible to bundle them all together under one title, which is: **the illness of duplexity and contradiction.**

Therefore, the overall, grave matter that the upcoming generation in our community is suffering from is nothing other than duplexity! There is duplexity in following an exemplar, duplexity in education, duplexity in pedagogy, and duplexity in the presentation of ideas and values. In summary, it is the duplexity that is in all the fields that have a hand in the formation of a young person's personality and his intellectual fabric. In the school – which is the most important pedagogical element – the student receives a mixture of contradictory and incompatible values and opinions – regarding ideas, approach and conduct – from competing and contradicting teachers and educators. What he receives from the teacher of philosophy and ethics is the opposite of what he receives from the teacher of religion, and what he receives from the science teacher differs from what he learnt from the first two.

The process of nurturing, education, and cultivation of the mind,[14] in the life of the student, becomes a struggle between building and demolishing and scrambling attempts, and the result in both his mind and soul is dust and dark veils that prevent the mind from thinking and the soul from finding any tranquillity. On the street, in the library, the club, in front of the television, he is surrounded by other examples of astonishing contradiction. In all of these facilities and institutions he hears about morals and virtues and the need to be bound by them and the danger of transgressing their rules. He also hears about freedom and the modern age and the need to adorn oneself with them, and about the danger of being repressed, shackled, and withdrawn in the mire of traditions.

In all of these facilities and institutions, he hears about the Religion along with its realities, its values, the need to establish a community based on its pillars, and to use its methods and treatments to solve every problem. However, he also hears about reactionism[15] and its flaws compared to the scientific renaissance and how the latter has abrogated religious beliefs, and about the need to liberate minds from the prison of faith in unseen matters and to use materialist thought to solve every problem and liberate every land!

He notices this grave contradiction in the street that he walks along, he reads it in the books and magazines that he peruses, and he hears it in the lectures and conferences that he goes to. Then he suffers it when he is with his friends and colleagues, upon whom he reflects

14 Ar. *at-tathqīf*.
15 Ar. *ar-rajaiyyah*, which can also be translated as backwardness, i.e. reacting to everything instead of initiating anything, and this is what Islam and Muslims are accused of.

all of it, in debates, arguments, and general commotion. Then at home the effects of all of that gather around him, and in ways that are more serious and harmful.

It is rare to see a family whose members do not disagree with one another, each one inclining towards one of these contradictory ideas and trends. Thus, the bliss and harmony of the home are turned into disunity and misery. The father has a bad relationship with his children. The wife's relationship with her husband becomes critical and dire. Loud arguments between all the members of the family take place every morning and evening.

Then this contradiction embodies itself in other aspects of the community, where it takes on a calm veneer of sleek hypocrisy. Thus, in its harms and tribulations for the upcoming generation, this contradiction outweighs all other contradictions, as those harms and tribulations alone usually claim the most victims: the young person listens, with a tranquil soul and sincere heart, to talk of patriotism and sacrifice, and it is delivered with splendid words and slogans, and thus he believes in it, he becomes passionate, and he starts to react to it. Then, unexpectedly, he realises that the matter is nowhere near how it is being described. It is actually nothing more than fancy words.

He then listens to many preachers, speakers, and guides and is affected by what he hears. Within his soul, he aspires to have exalted values and virtuous character, but not long after he has started making this effort with sincerity and keenness is he surprised to find that there are other motives and interests behind these profound speeches and lectures. He discovers that the state of those delivering them is the complete opposite.[16]

This is the community that the young person grows up in! This is the atmosphere in which he is nurtured and educated and in which he learns how to conduct himself. So what do you expect to become of this young person that is better than what people complain about now?

Who is the young person?

The young person is a fresh, ripe mass of a mind, soul, and emotions. Each of these three elements is in the greatest need of proper nourishment, upon which his development and maturation rely. If the nourishment – unfortunately – is what we have described, **what will the outcome be?**

The first outcome is that the young person will fall into a psychological fight, or indeed struggle. **As for the effects of this outcome,** they are that the young person has no trust or confidence in the community, and thus he derives no benefit from the community and the community derives no benefit from him. Thus, the young person is not fit to learn from the community and the community is not fit to nurture him and raise him. Instead, the young person becomes his own teacher, guiding himself by himself.

Then other outcomes appear after that, and there is no doubt that they are embodied in intellectual deviation, psychological complexity, and impulsive unrestraint.

---

16 This is not a judgment against all of them. Rather, it describes many of them, and their number is enough to paint the community in this unfortunate light.

Know that to the extent that there is contradiction and duplexity, which we have described as being ferocious and severe in the community, it will be ferociously and severely reflected in young people.

Look and you will see confirmation of this embodied in the disparity of what they call "the problem of the youth" today if you compare between the different communities of the world, and that is a consequence of the extent to which this illness has been aggravated therein.

Now, let us study the grave consequences which, in the end, are reflected in the young person's life after his psychological struggle, regardless of whether that struggle was long or short.

These dangerous consequences are first embodied in intellectual deviation, because contradictory logical premises only produce one result: **the rejection of the nature of logic itself.** Do not expect anything else from a young person as long as he is in the phase in which his intellect naturally relies on the opinions and teachings of others. He has relied on them and thus their confusion has left him with constant defectiveness in his thinking.

For him, what value does the intellect have left when you know that his standard for measuring that value is the reality of the community that he is living in? He has looked and seen that the intellect is thoroughly torn between astonishing contradictions. It is normal to find that most of these young people do not believe in anything, **because *nothing* is the logical outcome of a constant struggle between two things.**

The grave consequences are then embodied in psychological complexity, because the human psyche only makes its way through life because it is motivated by a combination of emotions that are motivating, deterring, and praising. These emotions are only woven into the psyche by the community and what it contains by way of motives of hope, expectation, and love, along with the deterrents of fear, punishment, apprehension and, finally, the means of comfort, luxury, and rewards.

To the extent that the soul has a balanced mix of these three kinds of human emotion, it will find tranquillity, bliss, and stability. So, how can a soul that has been fed and watered by a community like this have any sort of emotional balance or harmony?

The community in which different values, opinions, and schools of thought are interwoven and struggling with one another and when it treats the upcoming generation as an experimental field or arena for its struggles and conflicts – whether that is embodied in the school, the house, the street, or the library –; this community cannot nourish the young person's soul with any sense of love, hope, or expectation. Furthermore, it cannot connect it with any balanced mix of fear, apprehension, or a spirit of punishment.

The outcome is that this young person's soul comes to rebel against everything. It has no sense of loyalty, it is not guided by love, and it is not deterred by fear. It is a disturbed soul that does not even believe in itself, and is only nourished by its own selfishness. This is because it has looked to the authority of the intellect and not found anything that would obligate any other form of conduct. Furthermore, from what the community has offered, it has not found anything better to devote itself to.

Finally, these grave consequences are embodied in impulsive unrestraint, because when the intellect has been blunted and is unable to discern and restrain, and its ability to control and direct the soul has dwindled, natural impulses come to the fore, breaking out spontaneously.

It is human nature that the more a person is liberated from the shackles of his mind, the more committed he is to his impul-

sive motives. Were it not for the restraints of the mind and intellect, man would just be an animal with unbridled passions and desires; it would be rare to find another animal that has such petulance.

This is because the laws of impulse in animals are different and take the place of the intellect, as their lives depend on planned mental signals.[17]

As for man, his impulses are just burning urges and desires, because the intellect's existence and its shackles mean there is no need for his impulses to be regulated and planned. When the intellect is not there to provide wisdom and guidance, his impulses become inflamed, and you will find nothing like it in any animal.

These are the outcomes of the psychological struggle in young people, as it reflects the contradictions and duplexity of the community that we have described.

These outcomes are inevitable. There is no point in stubbornly denying them. Observable reality does not need any theoretical proof. The severity of these outcomes is proportionate to the severity of the contradictions that are present in the community, or it could be according to the young person's circumstances, how immersed in or detached from he is from this contradictory community.

We shall look at this second factor in detail later.

---

17 (tn): For example, an animal will only kill another animal in order to eat and will stop eating once it is full. It will not kill another animal for no reason or eat when it is not hungry. This is how an animal's impulses are regulated and planned.

The Problem of Social Pitfalls

This is a problem of another kind; it can stir up a struggle in the young person's soul just as we have described. However, it prevents him – partially or wholly – from moving towards the end that he believes in and deprives him of much of his ability to counter the impeding trends that he is exposed to.

In this brief work, we are not able to examine all of these problems, so we shall focus on elucidating the most important and comprehensive of them.

There are two serious problems that the young person from the community suffers from. Each of them represents a major pitfall standing in front of him. They transform his path towards uprightness and correct guidance into a difficult venture in which the possibilities of destruction are greater than the possibilities of safety and success.

The first of the two is what he faces in the crowded streets and markets and then in public facilities and institutions.

The second is what he faces within the walls of his own home when he comes together with members of his family.

On the street, the young person sees strange and stimulating sights that are focused on reducing all of his characteristics to one in particular, which is that he is a "sexual" animal; what he desires from this worldly life is one thing, which is sex. Once upon a time, these sights were regulated; they were governed by religion, honour, morality, the law, or the regime. Today, however, they are governed by one-way traffic. If, today, the traffic has reached the point of showing half of the thigh, tomorrow it will race towards showing the other half. The traffic is moving and the road is completely open. There is nothing to hinder it: not religion, not honour, not morality, not even taste!

This traffic is being pushed forward, and forward is whatever direction it is heading in. Of course, it might actually be moving backward, and there is nothing obstructing it. Rather, it is the young person who collides, because of the effects of this one-way traffic, with the fiercest and most furious obstacles within his own soul.

The young person wants to dedicate his entire essence to his entire existence, in harmony and balance. He dedicates his thoughts and his intellect to the secrets and realities of the universe. He dedicates his pride and his energy to the life that he enjoys and the land that he owns. He dedicates his feelings and his emotions to the truth that he believes in. He dedicates his human impulses to building the community and the procession of life. However, of the entire existence that surrounds him, he only encounters that which interacts with his human impulses.

Therefore, it is very natural – if this stream of sexual stimulation surrounds him for a period of time – for his entire essence to be reduced to that of a sexual animal. If you ask his intellect about the realities of the universe, his impulses will tell you that it is all about women! If you ask him why he is alive, he will tell you, with every fibre of his being, that it is to have an intimate night with a beautiful girl!

The problem is not that the young people in this age are more sexually stimulated than previous generations. That is a false understanding.

The problem, in fact, is that the community does not interact with any part of the young person's essence unless it is via his sexual impulse. It does not just wake it up but it stimulates it, with all kinds of temptations and excitants. At the same time, it prepares for all of his other human aptitudes and peculiarities more means of putting him into a deep slumber. The escalation and increase of sexual temptations have very serious consequences for the entire community that thinkers and researchers are rarely aware of.

The elucidation of this is that the means of temptation lose a large part of their effectiveness when people are exposed to them for a long period of time and become used to them. At that point, the means of temptation need to be intensified and expanded in order to renew their effectiveness and reignite their flame.

The matter continues like a vicious cycle; long exposure leads to weariness and boredom, which then, in turn, call for renewal. The means of temptation and stimulation are left of their own accord to enter an increasingly fierce competition with the means of boredom and obsoletion.

The competition continues and only stops when it reaches its natural limit, which is when gratification and pleasure can go no further. However, long exposure continues to implement its law until it reaches the peak of possible gratification and pleasure. The upcoming generation, who have seen everything and experienced everything, thus becomes bored and fed up. However, the soul keeps searching in a strange frenzy for novelty and new means of gratification.

This is why it is the start of insanity in its most dangerous form, dangerous to the community and to everything that is precious in life!

We have seen that the starting points of this insanity, or indeed many of its effects, in many parts of the Western world, and that its factors move with astonishing speed towards the most disastrous consequences for that entire world. We have also seen that our community is moving down the same path, and that the unrestricted competition between the means of sexual temptations and the means of boredom and weariness continues unabated with everything that it has; there is nothing to stop this suicidal competition, other than the natural end that is the starting point for abnormality, perversion, and insanity.

The young Muslim is faced with – from this grave social reality – a grave obstacle that cannot be overcome unless by way of something that resembles a miracle. It is an obstacle that prevents him from making his way to Allah. It is an obstacle that prevents him from mustering any type of defence of his land, his honour, or anything that he holds dear. It is an obstacle that prevents him from moving towards forming his essence and developing his humanity and perceptive faculties, because this obstacle, by its nature, melts all of these motives that are inside of him and fuses them into a singular, sexual impulse!

As for at home, he is faced with – in many cases – another pitfall of another type, but it is no less dangerous than the first type.

The elucidation of this is that the social reality, one aspect of which we have described, causes the family to be comprised of (in most cases) members who have differing leanings, orientations, and conduct, all of which is a reflection of the community's contradictions and duplexity and what each individual arrives at in his own venture with conflicting trends and currents.

As a result, what often happens is that this young man, or young woman, grows up while resisting these deviant trends and maintaining for himself an essence of the sound, human disposition. That disposition, in turn, is surrounded by faith in Allah and adherence to His Path. One of his parents, or both, or maybe all the members of the family, are disgusted by his uprightness and his religious behaviour and conduct, because all of that – according to what they have become accustomed to – falls under what is called abnormality, punctiliousness, introversion, and other similar terms. They all mobilise themselves against this poor person, and maybe the parents, or one of them, will use the vilest of means to make him renounce what his heart believes in, what his feelings have submitted to, and what his upright conduct is based on. They will thus deny him or her the most fundamental expenses and needs, such as food and clothing, even though Allah has blessed them with abundant wealth and ample sustenance.

Yes! This savage and astonishing opposition is not some foreign, colonialist epidemic, some Zionist mischief, or some foreign enemy of the Religion. Rather, it is opposition coming from "Muslim" parents, who repeat the motto of Islam on their tongues, and maybe the father goes to one of the masjids every now and then. Maybe both of them give the appearance of being "traditional" Muslims by the words and mottos they use.

And thus the young Muslim feels estranged, wherever he goes. I cannot imagine a tribulation that is worse than having one's own home, where one is supposed to find calm and tranquillity, turned into an element of opposition, and those who are in it, who are one's closest relatives, are turned into strangers and quarrelsome opponents!

In the best and most appropriate circumstances for this young person, the home is inevitably – apart from on rare occasions – far removed from any outward displays of Islam or Islamic etiquettes:

relatives and in-laws are constantly mixing and mingling,[18] time is killed by amusements that Allah is not pleased with and are of no benefit, parts of the body that must be covered[19] are exposed, and thus glances are stolen of disgraceful, unlawful sights that feed the excited soul with sinful dreams.

A home like this is not connected to any Islamic approach or Islamic manners in any way, and no young person in such a home will grow into the prime of his life upon Islam's polished, natural disposition. Furthermore, there is no doubt that a home like this, with the people who live in it, its circumstances, and its general environment, is a stranger to the young person who wants to maintain his manners and his religion.

This is why a young person like this cannot feel at home anywhere in his own home apart from in his small room, in which he seeks refuge and locks himself in. This is where he goes whenever he needs to relax, or to eat and drink. If he comes out of his room and sits and mingles with other household members, he exposes himself to the greatest threats: the loss of his essence, the effacement of guidance, and the deviation of conduct.

What troubles these young people the most is when they find themselves caught between exposing themselves to Allah's ﷻ anger and exposing themselves to the wrath of one of their parents or both. Thus, a young person could obey Allah's ﷻ command in his behaviour or in some aspect of his appearance and by doing so he will anger one of his parents. This will mean that he is disrespectful and disobedient to that particular parent. On the other hand, he could disobey Allah ﷻ and make little something that Allah has commanded or declared unlawful, and thus he is being respectful to his parents and both of them are pleased and happy with him.

18 (tn): i.e. between men and women who can lawfully marry.
19 Ar. *awrah*, i.e. the parts of the body that a man and a woman who can lawfully marry are not allowed to display in front of the other.

To solve this problem, it is not important for him to remember Allah's ﷻ words:

﴿وَإِن جَٰهَدَاكَ عَلَىٰٓ أَن تُشْرِكَ بِى مَا لَيْسَ لَكَ بِهِۦ عِلْمٌ فَلَا تُطِعْهُمَا ۖ وَصَاحِبْهُمَا فِى ٱلدُّنْيَا مَعْرُوفًا﴾

"But if they try to make you associate something with Me about which you have no knowledge, do not obey them. Keep company with them correctly and courteously in this world." [Luqmān 31:15]

Rather, it is important for him to be wise and adroit and thus obey Allah the Exalted without angering his parents, so that he can realise His ﷻ words: **"Keep company with them correctly and courteously in this world".**

These two difficulties are the tip of the social problems that the young person has to contend with on the way to forming himself and on the way to attaining his Lord's pleasure. The rest are branch problems that are beyond the scope of this study.

Treating These Problems

Maybe analysing these problems is something easy for the researcher, as there is no young person who is sincere with himself except that he is aware of these problems and lives with their causes and effects. Furthermore, maybe talking about how serious these problems are is easier and simpler, as there is no one who suffers from their trials except that he knows how badly they affect the community and the individuals and he can picture the horrific tragedy that will befall the Ummah as a result. No one denies this unless he is astonishingly stubborn.

Nevertheless, it is important to look for a treatment for these problems.

Sincere people from this Ummah are restlessly looking for a treatment that will eradicate these massive dangers or mitigate their impact, before catastrophe strikes and no treatment will be of any use.

However, when talking about the treatment and calling to it, whom do we address, the community and its leaders or young people and their families?

I told you at the beginning of this discussion: it is the community that is ill, not the youth, and the problems of the youth are only a symptom of the community's illness.

Therefore, the treatment must be presented to the community and not to one of its individuals.

However, I have also told you that talking about the problems of the youth might come to no avail, because those who are suffering from these problems do not possess any practical means of solving them.

And there has never been a day when speech alone has been able to do without means of implementation.

Nevertheless, I shall address my words of advice and warning to the community first. I shall place in front of them the remedy for this serious malady, and beyond that I have nothing but the agony and frustration of my soul and the sincerity of my heart.

If I do that, and I exhaust every effort in attempting to wake up the community and set it right, I shall then turn to the youth and draw their attention to a way that I know is not a treatment for their situation but is a form of passive resistance for which there is no alternative. It will help them against the dark affliction that cannot be avoided.

The first part of this section, therefore, will be an elucidation of the real treatment for these problems. It will be prescribed for the community in its composite form; it is not for the youth as individuals.

As for the second part, it will be, as I have told you, nothing more than drawing attention to passive resistance against a presumed catastrophe – and it is addressed only to the youth.

The Appropriate Treatment to Avert These Problems

Let us start by talking about the first part. Let us ask about the treatment that the community should take to avert these problems and put an end to them.

The answer is that there is only one treatment and no other, which is that the community be sincere with itself, and that its collective whole be in harmony with all of its parts and aspects.

'Ilm, thaqāfah, nurturing and thinking all have to be directed towards realising an objective that is not incongruent and does not contain confusion. There must be leadership that places the goal and the objective in the hands of *'ilm* alone, such that when demonstrative truths,[20] coming from ways of life and the schools of thought of researchers, point towards something specific therein, it is obligatory upon the community to make sure all of its institutions and facilities move in harmony with what those realities point to.

The attempt to uncover truth is the most sanctified thing a person can do, in any time or place. The only beacon that can accompany man at this stage is *'ilm*. Whenever *'ilm* leads man to the truth and discloses to him its enigmas and concomitants, it is at that point that there is nothing more sanctified for him to do than to subject his life to what that truth entails and to make civilisation a fortress that protects the intellect from straying away from truth after having found it.

A community's sanctified values – whether they are from a religion, morals, virtues and so forth – should not have any intrinsic value un-

---

20 Ar. *al-haqaa'iq al-'ilmiyyah*, which can also be translated as scientific realities/facts.

less they are in harmony with the greatest truth[21] that the beacon of ʿilm, and its law, has unveiled. Then, there should not be any confusion or incongruity between the values in the community, as long as all of them take shade under demonstrative truth[22] and seek refuge in its authority.

However, has the community taught its people the meaning of ʿilm? Has it ever drawn their attention to the great natural barriers that stand between demonstrative truth, which cannot be refuted, and suspicious theories and dubious hypotheses? Has it informed them that demonstrative truth is one and cannot differ with or contradict itself? Has it ever implanted in their minds or in the depths of their souls – at any stage of their upbringing and education – that demonstrative truth is the master of all human ends and objectives, and that all other goals are merely subsidiary branches of this main goal?

The community has not taught its individuals any of this. Instead, it has raised them upon the opposite, content to let the word ʿilm disseminate and be pompous for those who utter it and pleasant for those who hear it.

The people have learned from the community that each individual can use the word ʿilm for whatever idea he likes. Thus, ʿilm for the Marxist is whatever Marx and his followers say it is, such as the control of dialectical reproduction over the entire world. For others, ʿilm is according to the view that the world is based on a system of mechanical causes. For Darwinists, ʿilm is the view that living species evolve from one another. According to the agnostics, ʿilm is what the sophists regard as the necessity of abandoning the intellect and not relying on any of its judgments.

If this pandemonium indicates anything, it is that the word ʿilm is being abused and that individual doctrines, each espousing biases and

---

21 (tn): i.e. that Allah exists, that this universe has a Planner and to Him we shall return.
22 Ar. al-haqeeqah al-ʾilmiyyah, which can also be translated as scientific reality/fact.

personal objectives, are the axis of attitude and perception. It is not *'ilm* or demonstrative truth as they claim. Otherwise, their differing would force them to admit that demonstrative truth is buried somewhere else, far away from their arguments.

It is upon the community to draw its individuals' attention towards the correct way to seek the truth and to the standard by which facts are distinguished from pseudo-facts, to ingrain in them love of the truth because it is the truth, and, for that reason, to teach them how to read and why they read.[23]

It is well-known that our previous communities were concerned with this matter like no other community was. They carved a path for themselves towards knowing the truth (for itself and no other reason) in the middle of conflicts and struggles between differing sects and passions. The path to truth that they used was within the known limits of the scientific method in research and in accordance with the scales of logic, which, by their nature, distinguish between truth on the one hand and illusions and assumptions on the other.

Our previous communities, after that, started taking their individuals along that path. Nothing motivated them that was more sanctified than discovering the truth, and then ascertaining that it is the truth. Individuals received their nurturing and education on the basis of one, fundamental motto: **deliverance from error[24] is nothing other than knowing the truth and then acting in accordance with it in all institutions and facilities of life.**

---

23 I came across a treatise published by Dār al-Maʿārif in Egypt in which a group of researchers and thinkers respond to the question: **why do we read?** Unfortunately, I did not find a single one of them replying: 'We read, or we must read, in order to know the truth and then act accordingly.'

24 There is no doubt the book *al-Munqidh min ad-Ḍalāl* ('Deliverance from Error) by Imam al-Ghazālī is considered the most sublime embodiment of this path and guiding people to what is best.

If the truth has informed us that this universe is nothing other than the making of its Creator, that this Creator is not frivolous or inattentive in His creation, that He ﷻ has attached to this creation of his an elucidation that clarifies how man was created and why, what the function of every part or molecule of creation is and then what the function of man himself is, what the inseparable connection is between him and his Lord, and what his final destination – without doubt – will be.

It is clear that the veracity of this truth is not conditional on everyone's affirming it and believing it. **Rather, the first, sound condition** is that everyone who has a free and just intellect affirms it, those who do not burden their intellects at the start of the path with the chains of their own biases and desires. **The second condition** is that between this truth and the view of the intellect there be a sound approach of scientific research that, by its nature, distinguishes truth from that which resembles or masquerades as truth.

Our community today – with its internal incongruity and contradictions because of what we have mentioned – has no choice but to affirm this truth and submit to its authority. You should be able to see this from its general Islamic character, prevalent in all of its facilities and institutions as well as its schools and institutes, as well as many of its laws and ruling systems.

Therefore, let us go back to the question: **what is the treatment that will rectify the condition of our community?** And I have already told you: there is only one thing that will rectify the community's condition, which is that it be sincere with itself and that its collective whole be in harmony with all of its parts and aspects. The community will be rectified – and this is what Islam and its way affirm – when all of its apparatuses are in harmony and cooperating in this way.

Thus, the schools, with their various curricula, lessons, and systems, must combine their efforts in this way. **Cultural activity,** which is embodied in publishing books, journals, and the like as well as the productions of the **media**, must not slip or deviate from this way. **The values and principles** that the community professes must not, in any way, contradict the values and principles of Islam. Also, **the approach towards development and progress** must be confined to Islam's method and approach.

Yes, a young person's ears should not hear two contradictory discussions, one which constantly venerates Allah's signs and proofs and another that depreciates those same signs and proofs.

It should not be intimated to young men that those who harass young women are punished and those who deviate and pursue vice are debased and then those who intimate themselves encourage temptations of vice and applaud displays of nakedness, sex appeal, and other incitements to deviation!

The schools should not be left to be fields of competition for conflicting ideological tendencies alongside lessons of the Religion that students receive from a responsible teacher in a formal and organised manner.

No newspaper or journal should be a vehicle for publishing religious discussion, reminding people of their Creator and His reckoning, while at the same time it publishes discussions that mock the Religion, its proofs, and its restrictions.

A writer like me should not be exerting himself to find solutions to the problems of the youth while other people are dedicating themselves to aggravating and exacerbating these same problems.

There should not be values and principles that we affirm – as we have said – and then the *thaqāfah* that we rely on is an expression of the values of others; we take pride in our language and its literature and then we rely on the *thaqāfah* that aims to suppress this language and its literature! We take pride in our sublime history but then we borrow *thaqāfah* from people who portray our beautiful history as being backward and inferior!

We say all of this if the community is one that affirms Islam and its way, as we have said. As for when the community is one that seeks a path other than Islam, we must quickly offer an alternative!

What is the alternative that will protect the essence of our community, treat its problems, and realise its interests?

Any alternative to Islam will place the community in general, and the youth in particular, in greater jeopardy than the problem that we are not trying to extricate ourselves from.

The madness that has overcome the youth in America and vast swathes of Europe, such that it pushes huge numbers of them towards suicide and other huge numbers towards isolation and absolute beastliness. It is the madness of the void and being far removed from religion, since religion in their lives is nothing more than slogans that are repeated in places of worship and churches. As for the community, conduct, and the standards of investigation and research, they are completely removed from religion, its rulings, and its morals.

Maybe some of them dream of an alternative that is embodied in western civilisation! Maybe they think that this alternative will give the community new strength of character and solve many of its problems.

These people must realise, however, that the Muslims are perfectly capable of going against the principles of Islam and deviating from its straight path, which raised them to the peak of history. However, they will never be capable of attaining any strength of character or honourable life after this deviation and rebellion.

What will definitely happen, after an attempt to bring Western civilisation towards us, is that we will fall into a psychological void, and we will end up in a condition that will make us feel that no history is familiar to us, and all other nations will look at us in this way, that is, like parasites that bounce off the walls of the civilisations that we feed off of. Our souls will be burdened with inferiority complexes, and all of that will turn into a barrier between us and arriving at the fruits that we imagine and our desires yearn for.

This is because a nation's civilisation is nothing other than the sap of its *thaqāfah*. A nation's *thaqāfah* is nothing other than the intellectual fruits of the values, beliefs and customs that have been agreed upon, as well as whatever past and history it has moved away from and the circumstances and problems it is moving towards.

It is therefore certain that importing Western civilisation, or the civilisation of any nation other than our own, means importing that nation's history, its circumstances, and the values that it relies on, so that it can take the place of its counterpart in our own lives. Is this not like someone who uses his friend's ID card so that he can benefit from it instead of his own? Is there any doubt, as a result of all of this, that the Ummah will inevitably fall into endless psychological contradiction and struggles? It is inevitable that it will destroy its intellectual clarity and its logical standards. It is inevitable that the residue of all of that will come together and form a calamitous malady that will stick to the youth, who are the vanguard of the Ummah, the sinew of strength and creativity!

These people must wake up to the fact that they are **desiring an alternative to Islam, not that they feel the need for an alternative, and there is a big difference between the two.**

The path of desiring is easy; it is followed by intelligent people as well as others, because its motive is from his natural inclination, and man is no different from animals in this regard. If man's natural inclination were to desire the rectification of that which is corrupt, probity would appear in the animal world. As for those who are seeking an alternative, because they feel the need for it, let them ask their intellects and their experiences about it, and the factual evidence of the world around them. Let them consider the wretchedness of the West and its civilization, and the world's lamenting its youth. Then, let them say, sincerely and objectively, **that they have found an alternative to Islam**.

***

Finally, this is the real remedy for the problems of the youth, and the community should take it in its composite form, as I have said.

I have described it and presented it in brief; I do not know whose ears in the community it will reach, nor do I know whether discussion about it will spread the way a cry spreads through a valley. I do not know if someone will come along who will be moved by some remnants of solicitude for this Ummah within him, and will thus reflect on what I have said freely and objectively and then work towards implementing the remedy with persistent striving and appropriate wisdom.

I do not know, but this is the utmost that I can do to treat the problem, and it may well be that Allah will cause a new situation to develop.[25]

---

25 See Sūrat at-Ṭalāq 65:1.

The Treatment of Resistance and Resilience

If the treatment does not find anyone who will use it, and the calamity is inevitable, there is no choice but to fortify the place that the calamity is heading towards, surrounding it with whatever means of resistance and protection are available.

Modifying the circumstances and conditions could be something that we are not capable of, for one reason or another, but what we are definitely capable of is rising above these circumstances and conditions and fortifying our psyches and our minds against their fallouts and their evil conditions.

And so forth, for it is incumbent upon the youth who disseminate their various complaints and ask writers and researchers about their abstruse problems to presume that the community will not listen and pay attention to their complaints, and it will not treat itself for the illness whose various banes are reflected in their lives. At that point, they have no choice but to rise above the community, and adopt whatever means they can to rid themselves of its contagion and protect themselves against its afflictions.

It is a path that is possible and easy if the young person adopts it freely and willingly to guide his conduct in life. When the young person succeeds in this resistive approach, he does not reap the benefits of that for only himself. Rather, its benefits extend to the community as well, because the passive, reserved stance that the young person enjoys in situations like this reflects another way of pushing and coercing the community to rectify its state and treat its maladies.

Let us examine and analyse these defensive ways and clarify how to benefit from them, one by one.

One: Problems Connected to 'Ilm and Thaqāfah

You know from what we have discussed that the words *'ilm* and *thaqāfah* are among the most important matters that the educated young person is infatuated with today. This is why he tries to read a lot, and he will read in any fashion, regardless of who the author, scholar, or scientist is.

This infatuation should actually be considered something noble, something that adorns a young person, not a defect or a disgrace! However, the matter has become something different from what it originally was because the circumstances are different, and depending on the different paths that a young person wants to follow in order to realise his desire or his voracity for knowledge.

It is incumbent upon the young person to know that most materials that are put out by printing presses nowadays, such as books and other publications that research all kinds of knowledges, facts, sciences, do nothing more than reflect the confusion of their authors regarding what they are trying to discuss and research. At best, they reflect nothing more than fragmentary studies of a range of knowledges, the researchers of which only made it halfway, or maybe a third of the way, and thus they are more of a danger to scientific truth than they are a facilitation or means of arriving at it.

Likewise, the young person must know that we are in the age of trade, trading in everything, and perhaps "the commodity of the book" is one of the bestselling commercial commodities in our markets. Surely the salesman is the most dangerous enemy to the truth and the acid that is quickest at melting it, transforming it, veiling it, or ruining it, regardless of how sanctified and venerated its roots are.

The young person therefore – before devoting himself to reading and diving into all kinds of books – must learn the art of choosing the topic, then the art of choosing the book, and then know how to read and follow research.

The mistake of spontaneity in choosing a subject matter of knowledge is no less serious than the mistake of spontaneity in choosing to study and research one issue from among several issues that fall under one subject.[26]

In other words, it is not possible to digest a subject matter in a healthy fashion unless the research is done gradually, starting with the preliminaries and then each issue in its proper order: the first, the second, the third, and so forth. Likewise, a comprehensive study of a range of knowledges or sciences cannot be done properly unless one starts with that which is most general and comprehensive and then gradually narrows down to the most specific.

This is because the relationship of the various knowledges and sciences[27] have with one another is of no less important than the relationship that the issues of one discipline have with one another. Thus, just as the issues of one discipline are considered complementary to one another, the sum total of the various sciences and knowledges is considered a path towards one scientific, integrated truth.

---

26 (tn): i.e. one has to understand how the various issues of one subject are connected to one another.

27 I remind the reader that we mean knowledge in the general, unqualified sense, including the natural sciences and other sciences.

For example, someone who is devoted to the study of history but has no certain knowledge regarding the universe, man, and life might have some knowledge of history and its epochs, but his ideas are fragmented and distorted regarding the reality of existence and its primal, intrinsic factors. Most of these fragments continuously come into his mind because of the theology of whatever historian he is reading, while the rest are because he has mistakes regarding events or in his historical analyses of events.

You must know that the modern approach towards writing history obligates the author to cram his theology and his conceptions, which are the product of his own circumstances, into the explanation and analysis of historical events, regardless of how impartial he is required to be in his analysis and research.

It is therefore inevitable that someone who studies history before acquiring sufficient knowledge about the reality of the universe, man, and life will become a victim, because of his ignorance, of that historian's mentality and beliefs, and he will not even know it.

Another example would be someone who devotes himself to studying the Islamic Revealed Law, and comparing it and evaluating it, before acquiring sufficient knowledge of the life and times of Muḥammad 🕌 from the original, scientific sources; he will inevitably arrive at a dead end in his analysis, and, as a result, he will inevitably attack it with false conceptions and baseless rulings.[28]

For example, he is not able – because he has not studied the Prophetic Biography properly – to imagine that the Islamic Revealed Law is a suspended law, floating between the sky and the earth. It has no attribution that binds it to the sky nor any roots that tie it to any of the nations of the earth.[29] It was found this way, complete and integrated,

---

28 (tn): i.e. he will fabricate things, including rulings.
29 (tn): i.e. it is not from any created thing, whether in the sky or on earth.

in the desert of the Arabian Peninsula. He is therefore compelled – in order to solve this problem – to try to attribute it to the Jews at some point in time, and then try Roman Law at another time, without being aware that with this hypothesis he is falling into the most severe ignorance within the topic that he is studying in order to try to arrive at some authentic knowledge regarding it. If, when studying a topic, he were to give precedence to the root over the branch and study it first, he would not be confused and he would not find himself at a dead end.

Yet another example would be someone who studies the story of man's origin and development before studying the origin of the universe in its totality and without researching Allah's existence and that He is the creator of the universe. This person will inevitably fall into perpetual bewilderment instead of arriving at the knowledge that will put his soul at ease.

He will read therein the opinions of Lamarck, who presumed that all species were once compounded in one species, after which they differed and became dissimilar due to the effects of their surroundings and environment and their various organic needs. However, just before he is about to grasp those opinions, he will see them submerged by a flood of criticism.

After that, he will study another theory called Darwinism, which holds the view that man developed from a simple organism based on the law of the survival of the fittest. However, just as he is about to comprehend it, he will be surprised by another inundation of criticism and stinging refutation: by whose standard is the fittest determined, and on what basis is the fit distinguished from the unfit?

Where is this law when we see a nature that causes vast swamps to dry or unleashes horrible floods that result in millions of lives being extinguished, creatures who could have carried on living since they were protected by both strength and fitness?

Indeed, where is this law when we can see in this vast world that there are all kinds of creatures, from the smallest molecules, which are weak and unfit, through to the fittest and strongest specimens, and the fit among them do not remove the unfit from existence?

He ends up studying the criticisms, for which there is no answer, and then notices a third theory called Neo-Darwinism, which says: let us affirm that man developed randomly on the basis of mutational jumps, not on the basis of progressing towards becoming the fittest.

However, for a third time, criticism comes and says: why does man not jump backwards once instead of always pouncing forward? Why does he not take just one jump in a straight line towards realising an ultimate, designed cause, when all intelligent people know that an ultimate cause requires the most complicated processes of organisation and planning? What does the young person who studies in this manner come to understand? What scientific truth does he obtain?

As you have seen, he has only come across intellectual defences, the latest of which refutes the one that preceded it, and all of them are subject to bare criticism that no researcher is unaware of. It is an unavoidable dead end, and there is no escape from such confusion as long as the researcher does not start, before anything else, by studying the issues that are more comprehensive and general and following the natural or scientific sequence, which is no other than researching the greater origin of the universe as well as researching Allah's ﷻ existence and His being the creator of the universe.

If he had studied this as his first research, he would have arrived at an established fact that would have given him the key to unlocking the secrets of the second research, and that would have saved him from that perpetual bewilderment from which there is no escape.

In the course of all of this, I want to draw your attention to the fact that the cosmic knowledges and sciences, however they may appear to differ from one another, are actually connected to one another in a sequential manner, and there is no way for you to conceive any of this properly unless you start by knowing the principle that comes first and is the most comprehensive.

There is no doubt that the greatest principle, from which all branch knowledges and sciences are derived, is contemplating Allah the Exalted's existence and that He is the creator of the universe, such that when the researcher has arrived at certainty in that regard, it gives him certainty regarding the scientific matters that follow and are connected to it.

It is therefore incumbent upon the young person who wants to learn to be fully aware of the need to put subject matters in their proper, scientific order, and to dedicate himself – before everything else – to studying the knowledge that is the key to all the various sciences and knowledges, and that knowledge is nothing other than the knowledge that looks into Allah's existence, His attributes, and related matters.

Notice that I am not saying that the young person must have firm conviction. **Rather, I am saying** that he must study, as there is no good in a belief that is not bound together by the ties of ʿilm. If he submits to ʿilm and lets it lead him, it is not incumbent upon him that ʿilm lead him to any decision or firm conviction.

It is incumbent upon him, however, to study on the basis of a clear scientific approach, i.e. the scientific approach that does not mix actual ʿilm with theories, hypotheses, doubts, and illusions. The researchers who study in this manner must desire to know the pure truth, wherever it may be and however it may be, and not let their research be bogged down by agendas, biases, or personal interests and desires.

Of course, the young person will hasten to ask at this point: what writings, then, should I rely on in order to organise my knowledge journey, and with which researchers will I find the pure scientific approach that is not surrounded by any agenda or desire?

The answer is that if finding these researches and writings were easy, we would not be discussing what is called the problem of *'ilm* and *thaqāfah* right now.

As I have already told you, most materials that are put out by printing presses nowadays that research knowledges and sciences do nothing more than reflect the confusion of their writers and authors regarding the subject matter they are treating, even if that confusion dons the garb of scientific rules and dyes itself in definiteness and certainty.

You now know that the reason for this is the lack of paying attention to and observing the historical sequence in the study of knowledges and sciences and how they are linked to one another in a particular order. This is a bane that most writers and readers fall into, and in equal measure.

I have also told you that today we are in the age of trade, and that books are now one of the bestselling commodities in both our intellectual and economic markets.

You now know that one of the most important reasons behind this is that most of those who write and publish only do so as a means to promote some school of thought that they fanatically cling to, to realise some benefit that they are seeking, or to satisfy some grudge that they secretly bear. As for arriving at pure scientific truth, this is the last of their worries and concerns.

And this is the problem that we are talking about.

However, if the problem refuses to go away, is that, then, an excuse for the youth to use it as a knife to slaughter themselves with?

In this situation, there is no option for them other than to seek refuge from it by adopting a stance of resilience and resistance as much as possible.

That can only be by studying, before everything else, the scientific approach to looking for the truth, which is something that the majority of writers and knowledge merchants today pay no attention to. This means that they arm themselves with a proper study, starting with the most comprehensive and most fundamental of knowledges and sciences, which is researching the Creator's existence, and the extent to which this universe is connected to its Maker 餐.

Then, when studying this greatest principle leads one of them to free scientific certainty, he can study whatever lies beyond that, such as history, natural history, the story of man's development, and so forth, and he adheres therein to the rules of the scientific approach to looking for the truth,

Of course, embarking upon this path is an arduous task, akin to extracting silk threads from the branches of thorns, or extracting gold ore from the boulders and soil of mountains. However, in order to know the truth, the young person must be patient.

And he can take inspiration from those who have greater patience, such as those who plunge into the depths of the ocean to obtain a pearl or descend into a deep, rocky valley in order to obtain a handful of gold.

And he will find some of his colleagues striving towards the same objective and being patient in their research just as he is being patient, and by working with them the hardships he faces will be mitigated to a great extent and the path will be illuminated with lamps of energy and brotherhood.

I will not speak to you at length about the road that the young person should travel when facing these problems of *thaqāfah*, for it resembles what the young person should do when facing the problems of *'ilm* that we have discussed.

It is incumbent upon him not to forget the difference that we have mentioned between *thaqāfah* and *'ilm*. The truths of *'ilm* enjoy intrinsic independence and are not altered or modified from one nation to the next, nor are they influenced by custom, environment, or pedagogy.

As for matters of *thaqāfah*, they are aptitudes and faculties that take control of the mind and character and they are the product of what a nation enjoys by way of values, history, and foundations in pedagogy, thought, and way of living. There is no doubt that a *thaqāfah* can either be in harmony with and close to scientific truth or it can be the opposite, depending on the state of that nation and its civilisational view of life and its fruits.

When the young person has grasped this difference, he can then grasp what is called the problem of *thaqāfah* and become aware of how important and serious it is.

At that point, he will look at the community and see nothing other than incompatible shreds of the *thaqāfahs* of others, which our history is being pulled towards with ropes of force and coercion. These shreds are being imposed upon our language, regardless of how different it is, and exposing it to ruin and obliteration. Our literature and our pedagogical approaches are garbed in them regardless of how much contradiction and duplexity they produce. **There is no doubt that if you can conceive of the problem, you are halfway to solving it** – as they say.

In other words, if the young person grasps this, and he becomes determined not to fall victim to this corrupt intermixture, and he is strongly motivated to establish barriers between himself and the *thaqāfahs* of others, between what others possess and what we cherish of the fountainhead of civilisation, our history, our literature, our language, our values...provided that as an equivalent for that there would be a network of knowledge connecting between our *thaqāfah* and the lives of other nations, such that we would only take from them what is of pure scientific benefit and use it to nourish the institutions of our community and our way of life.

There is no doubt that this is another endeavour; it is not any easier and it is no less of a struggle against ostracism and isolation than the first endeavour that we outlined, which is how to rid oneself of the problems connected to *'ilm*. Nevertheless, it is an endeavour that is possible. It enjoys extraordinary suitability and usefulness, because it leads to the desired result and will mitigate the difficulties that surround it. No young person should imagine that he is alone in striving towards this objective. Rather, he is one individual of many just like him who are striving for the same thing, persevering just as he is persevering, and is not the community a collective of similar individuals?

The only obligation upon him is to carry out his urgent endeavour so that the number of these individuals multiplies. After some time, the problem will be isolated from the community, and will barely enjoy any authority or influence over it.

Two: The Problem of the Psychological Struggle

I told you before that the psychological struggle is the product of various maladies, but all of them fall under what I have called **the malady of duplexity and contradiction.**

If this malady refuses to do anything other than wreak havoc on the community, and if the physician[30] refuses to do anything but leave it so that he can monitor its aggravation and dangerous effects from nearby, **what, then, is the duty of the youth, who are the chaff and debris of that fire?**

We return once again to explain the means of resistance and the stance of protection and resilience, which is the only available means in this situation.

In this situation, the young person can do nothing but seek refuge in one of the lifeboats. The lifeboats in the vast ocean of this contradictory and duplex community are nothing other than the smaller communities that, by their nature, will protect him to a certain extent from the banes of that vast, heaving ocean of contradictions.

However, the path to seeking refuge in these lifeboats **is divided into two categories:**

As for the first category, its provision and preparation goes back to the parents.

As for the second, it is the responsibility of the young person himself, and I do not think that either of the two are independent of the other by any means. The most important of these small communities and the most capable in providing protection and defence is the home,

---

30 (tn): In this case, the 'physician' is those in the community who are aware of the problem and are in a position to do something about it.

but it is also possible for the matter to be inverted, and thus, in addition to not providing any defence or protection, the influence of the home is worse than that of the tumultuous ocean that he is fleeing from. And it is the parents who determine which of these two directions the home moves in.[31]

Yes, there is no doubt that when both parents come together upon morals, the Religion, and sound cultural awareness in order to regulate each other's lives, it has an extraordinary effect on the child in terms of guiding him and controlling his conduct and inclinations. There is no doubt that the child who grows up in this home will have a sound upbringing that will make him keep his distance from the external community, let alone be influenced by it.

This is because in the home he has that which nourishes his mind, his spirit, and his emotional life, and therefore his heart finds intimacy, his soul finds tranquillity, and his spirit finds calm. This is what gives him full confidence in the home and makes him happy to comply with it, naturally and fundamentally. If he ever looks out onto the reality of the tumultuous community around him, he will be surprised by it because it is not familiar to him; his nature and disposition will cause him to reject it. His small community of the home will be the strongest refutation of it and the clearest evidence that it is wrong.

When the child grows up and has reached young adulthood and intellectual maturity, those same pedagogical values and foundations grow up with him. Because of his maturity and intellectual independence, those values and foundations will be renourished and have more strength and resilience. However, now that he has outgrown his small nest and he is contending with the insolent and ferocious community,

---

31 (tn): the parents can provide protection and defence or they can provide the exact opposite.

he will need other small communities that are of a different type that he can seek refuge in, in times of adversity and in whom he will find stability and firmness.

This is all there is to it, if the child is fortunate and is blessed with righteous parents in the way that we have described.

If, on the other hand, the parents are victims of this fragmented, contradictory society, the child will have no option – especially when he is very young – but to submit to the approach that he is made to follow, that is, until he grows up and is able to think for himself.

It is at this point that the role of the second category of small communities comes in. This second category can be embodied in many different forms. It could be a group or selection of friends all of whom have excellent character and upright conduct, and they sincerely work together to meet the needs of this young person and his various psychological and social aspirations, and they will do so directly or, if they cannot help him with a particular matter, they will compensate.[32] This can also be in the form of a sincere guide[33] who is surrounded by sincere brethren or students, and thus he spends his entire life with his shaykh and in the company of his brethren and his companions.

Small communities like these, when the young person relies on them, bring about two benefits:

The first is that they show him – in an applied, tangible fashion – the correction of those mistakes and deviations that the surrounding community is dyed in. It refutes the illusion of those who say that the current state of the community is – regardless of its nature and its effect – is inevitable, and that any hope of rising above it is just "idealism" and not at all applicable.

---

32 (tn): i.e. they will find someone who can.
33 Ar. *murshid*.

The reality of the small world he lives in and whose authority he is under confirms for him every day the ridiculousness of this illusion. Right in front of him is a model of a community that is sincere with itself, whose parts are in harmony with one another, and right next to is a community that is incongruent, whose parts are consuming one another, and in which contradictions and hypocrisy have spread everywhere. Then the short-term and long-term effects of each one shows him profound harms or immense benefits.

What this means is that this comparison that this young person is constantly living, and seeing the contradictions of the larger community, pushes him to have more faith in and become more attached to the small community that he resides in. He will not be able to look at any hypocrisy or duplexity in the larger community without it making him feel more attached to the sincerity and uprightness in the smaller one.

And therefore, instead of this young person's falling victim to the contradictory values that the larger surrounding community embraces and becoming negative and confused to the extent that he disbelieves in everything that his small environment pushes him to seek shade in, he is positive and disbelieves in the lies and the hypocrisy in order to believe in uprightness, veracity, and sincerity.

And it is a permanent maxim in the life of man: when the life that surrounds him is full of contradictions and errors, it will be reflected as confusion and restlessness in his thinking and in his soul.

However, when he can see two distinct images, one showing contradiction and incongruity, with its various problems and corrosive effects and the other showing harmony and unity upon uprightness and sincerity, with its various positive and observable effects, it makes it easier for him to distinguish between truth and falsehood, and then it is easier for him to be attached to the latter and feel repelled by the former.

That is the first benefit.

As for the second benefit, it is that these small communities are righteous. They – after everything we have mentioned – will instil a spirit of brotherhood in his soul and he will not even feel the alienation of the isolation that he imposed upon himself, the withdrawal from the filth of the community, and remaining aloof from its storms and commotions.

This is because in the group, or the brethren or friends that fill the emptiness of his soul, or the righteous, sincere guide whose spirituality penetrates his heart, is the best compensation for the brotherhood and intimacy he needed from the community and from his family.

This is why I find myself repeatedly compelled, on every occasion, to draw attention to how important friendship and friends are in the life of the young Muslim. I have no doubt that a few friends who are sincere and wise have more effect and influence on a young person's life than heavy loads of knowledge and long hours of spiritual counsel and guidance.

The opposite, however, is also true. A group of friends can pulverise whatever maturity and good sense a young person has over the course of only two late night parties.

In a person's life, the connections of friendship are a bridge of immense importance; it will either lead a person to bliss and goodness or toss him into a blaze of misguidance and misery.

Three: The Problem of Social Pitfalls:

I have confined the discussion about these to two main problems:

The first is the problem of sexual stimulation in the streets and marketplaces.

The other is the problem of contradictions in the home, which can lead to war and conflict.

We have said that these two massive problems have branches and consequences and that we do not need to discuss them if we are successful in treating their two serious foundations.

Let us suppose that these pitfalls refuse to do anything other than remain and cause mischief in the community. What is the path of resistance that the young Muslim can follow in order to protect himself?

At this point, I am compelled to address my words exclusively to the youth who have true faith in Allah ﷻ. As for the others, there is no benefit in discussing this with them, because I do not know of any way to protect them or treat them.

I say the following to the former group:

As for expecting these pitfalls to go away and to be removed from your path, this is a big mistake in understanding the Divine Law of the universe. You can easily become aware of this by contemplating the Exalted One's words:

﴿مَّا كَانَ ٱللَّهُ لِيَذَرَ ٱلْمُؤْمِنِينَ عَلَىٰ مَآ أَنتُمْ عَلَيْهِ

حَتَّىٰ يَمِيزَ ٱلْخَبِيثَ مِنَ ٱلطَّيِّبِ﴾

"Allah will only leave the believers in the position you now are in so that He can sift out the rotten from the good". [Āl 'Imrān 3:179]

71

He ﷻ has also said:

﴿أَحَسِبَ ٱلنَّاسُ أَن يُتْرَكُوٓا۟ أَن يَقُولُوٓا۟ ءَامَنَّا وَهُمْ لَا يُفْتَنُونَ ۝ وَلَقَدْ فَتَنَّا ٱلَّذِينَ مِن قَبْلِهِمْ ۖ فَلَيَعْلَمَنَّ ٱللَّهُ ٱلَّذِينَ صَدَقُوا۟ وَلَيَعْلَمَنَّ ٱلْكَـٰذِبِينَ﴾

"Do people imagine that they will be left to say: 'We believe' and will not be tested? We tested those before them so that Allah would know the truthful and would know the liars". [al-'Ankabūt 29:2-3]

And He ﷻ has also said:

﴿زُيِّنَ لِلنَّاسِ حُبُّ ٱلشَّهَوَٰتِ مِنَ ٱلنِّسَآءِ وَٱلْبَنِينَ وَٱلْقَنَـٰطِيرِ ٱلْمُقَنطَرَةِ مِنَ ٱلذَّهَبِ وَٱلْفِضَّةِ وَٱلْخَيْلِ ٱلْمُسَوَّمَةِ وَٱلْأَنْعَـٰمِ وَٱلْحَرْثِ ۗ ذَٰلِكَ مَتَـٰعُ ٱلْحَيَوٰةِ ٱلدُّنْيَا ۖ وَٱللَّهُ عِندَهُۥ حُسْنُ ٱلْمَـَٔابِ﴾

"To mankind the love of worldly appetites is painted in glowing colours: women and children, and heaped-up mounds of gold and silver, and horses with fine markings, and livestock and fertile farmland. All that is merely the enjoyment of the life of this world. The best homecoming is in the presence of Allah". [Āl 'Imrān 3:14]

Man's slavehood to Allah ﷻ, therefore, is based on confronting the obstacles in his path, being patient with them, and then overcoming them in order to achieve Allah's ﷻ pleasure.

However, these obstacles can be less severe and fewer in number, and that is when they are under the shade of an Islamic community. That is when the burden of perseverance and patience is mitigated. At the same time, they can be more severe and greater in number when the effectiveness of the Islamic community is curtailed, and that is when the burden of perseverance and patience is heavy, and the reward – as the Messenger of Allah ﷺ has said – is according to one's toil and effort.[34]

You are in an age in which Allah has written for those who are upright and adhering to Allah's path a reward that is like those of the truly sincere and the martyrs in the time of the Prophet ﷺ, since they had people who helped them adhere to the truth and you do not have such people. Their patience, therefore, for the sake of the truth was less severe and bitter than your patience today.

That does not mean, however, that those who deviate from the truth today have an excuse such that they are liable to less severe punishment than those like them who came before. This is because reward is anchored in perseverance and patience, and therefore, the greater the patience, the greater the reward.

Bearing sin, on the other hand, is anchored in indulging in what Allah the Exalted has declared unlawful, regardless of what the means are that lead to the unlawful. It is not for anyone to complain about the roughness and difficulty of his own road as long as he is able to have patience, and as long as his reward differs from that of others according to the extent of his patience and its intensity.

The upshot of these words is that the best protection that the believer can fortify himself with against the stimulations and pitfalls of the community is patience, as it is the axis and foundation of all divine commands. Have you not seen Allah's ﷻ words:

﴿يَـٰٓأَيُّهَا ٱلَّذِينَ ءَامَنُواْ ٱصْبِرُواْ وَصَابِرُواْ وَرَابِطُواْ وَٱتَّقُواْ ٱللَّهَ لَعَلَّكُمْ تُفْلِحُونَ﴾

---

34 Ar. ʿalā qadar in-naṣab.

"You who believe, be patient; be supreme in patience, be firm on the battlefield; and have *taqwā* of Allah, so that perhaps you will be successful". [Āl 'Imrān 3:200]

It is inevitable that the young person will rush to ask: **but how can I be patient?**

You should know, dear reader, that this question is nothing more than a clever formulation of another question. The correct formulation is: **but is there a way to attain Allah's pleasure that does not require patience?**

The answer is that there is no way to achieve Allah the Exalted's pleasure that does not require adversity and patience. It is useless and futile to look for a way to enter Paradise that is easy, that matches our own desires and wishes. This is what Allah's will has made necessary, and nothing thwarts His rule and His will.

However, you should also know that the ways of slavehood to Allah the Exalted are numerous and varied, and from them emerges another form of assistance.

In other words, when the Religion has become complete in a person's life and he adheres to all of its rules and regulations, that will assist him in subjecting his passions and desires to Allah's ﷻ rulings.

If his thoughts and feelings are only alert and awake to one aspect of the Religion, such that he neglects all the other aspects, he will find great difficulty in trying to keep hold of that one aspect.

There is, therefore, only one thing that will help the Muslim have patience, which is to have all the aspects of Islam complete and integrated into his life. This is a fact that is repeated more than once in Allah's Book:

Have you not seen His ﷻ words:

$$﴿ وَمَن يَتَّقِ ٱللَّهَ يَجْعَل لَّهُ مَخْرَجًا ۞ وَيَرْزُقْهُ مِنْ حَيْثُ لَا يَحْتَسِبُ .....$$

$$..... ۞ وَمَن يَتَّقِ ٱللَّهَ يَجْعَل لَّهُ مِنْ أَمْرِهِ يُسْرًا ۞ ذَٰلِكَ أَمْرُ ٱللَّهِ أَنزَلَهُۥ إِلَيْكُمْ ۚ وَمَن يَتَّقِ ٱللَّهَ يُكَفِّرْ عَنْهُ سَيِّئَاتِهِۦ وَيُعْظِمْ لَهُۥ أَجْرًا ﴾$$

"Whoever has *taqwā* of Allah, He will give him a way out, and provide for him from where He does not expect... Whoever has *taqwā* of Allah, He will make matters easy for him. That is Allah's command that He has sent down to you. Whoever has *taqwā* of Allah, He will erase his bad actions from him and greatly increase his reward". [at-Ṭalāq 65:2-5]?

He ﷻ has also said:

$$﴿ مَنْ عَمِلَ صَالِحًا مِّن ذَكَرٍ أَوْ أُنثَىٰ وَهُوَ مُؤْمِنٌ فَلَنُحْيِيَنَّهُۥ حَيَوٰةً طَيِّبَةً ﴾$$

"Anyone who acts rightly, male or female, while being a believer, We will give them a good life". [an-Naḥl 16:97]

Thus, the one who is being sexually stimulated and cannot be patient with what Allah has commanded must go back to having faith in the Last Day and the reckoning and reward therein, and reinforce that faith and renew it. The only thing that is depriving him of the means of patience is either doubt or some weakness that has afflicted his certainty in the Day of Recompense. Whenever a person increases in his certainty in this day, his heart senses it more and is more in awe of it. As a result, his capacity for patience and resilience will also increase.

Then, after that, he must use this faith that he has a ladder to arrive at Allah's U pleasure, and to empty his heart of everything besides Him, and thus he desires nothing but His grace and fears nothing but His power.

The way to achieve this is to realise that all the formative elements of his existence, his life, his happiness, and his comfort are by Allah's ﷻ grace alone. Everything else that this worldly life is replete with, the well-coordinated creatures and creations that have been made to serve man, are one of the most prominent manifestations of Allah's generosity and solicitude towards him. Every blessing that Allah confers upon you for you to enjoy can easily be transformed – by His will – into a trial that destroys you.

Water, which Allah has made the secret of your life, can easily become a means of your destruction, if He willed such. The air that you inhale and that circulates within you can, if He so wills, can become a devastating hurricane. The earth, which Allah the Exalted has prepared for you to live on and is the source of your food and drink; Allah can, if He so wills, turn it into a chasm that swallows you or magma that spits you out.

The animals that Allah subjugated for you to ride and plough with; if Allah wanted, He could grant them permission to be fearsome beasts that subjugate man instead of the other way around.

If you would like to, listen and pay attention to the elucidation of this fact in Allah's ﷻ words:

﴿ءَأَمِنتُم مَّن فِى ٱلسَّمَآءِ أَن يَخْسِفَ بِكُمُ ٱلْأَرْضَ فَإِذَا هِىَ تَمُورُ ۝ أَمْ أَمِنتُم مَّن فِى ٱلسَّمَآءِ أَن يُرْسِلَ عَلَيْكُمْ حَاصِبًا فَسَتَعْلَمُونَ كَيْفَ نَذِيرِ﴾

"Do you feel secure against Him who is in the sky causing
the earth to swallow you up when suddenly it rocks from
side to side? Or do you feel secure against He who is in
the sky releasing against you a sudden squall of stones,
so that you will know how true My warning was?"
[al-Mulk 67:16-17]

Or His ﷻ words here:

﴿أَوَلَمْ يَرَوْاْ أَنَّا خَلَقْنَا لَهُم مِّمَّا عَمِلَتْ أَيْدِينَآ أَنْعَـٰمًا فَهُمْ لَهَا مَـٰلِكُونَ ۝
وَذَلَّلْنَـٰهَا لَهُمْ فَمِنْهَا رَكُوبُهُمْ وَمِنْهَا يَأْكُلُونَ ۝ وَلَهُمْ فِيهَا مَنَـٰفِعُ وَمَشَارِبُ
أَفَلَا يَشْكُرُونَ﴾

"Have they not seen how We created for them, by Our
own handiwork, livestock which are under their control?
We have made them tame for them and some they ride
and some they eat. And they have other uses for them,
and milk to drink. So will they not be thankful?"
[Yā Sīn 36:71-73]

When this fact has been made clear to you and you live in its shade,
contemplating it and reflecting on it, intense love for Allah will ripen in
your heart along with immense awe of Him ﷻ, and it will not be long
before that spreads throughout your entire essence.

The lover – as you know – always strives to please his beloved. He
bears with every adversity and spares no effort, and not just patiently
but happily and elatedly.

What can sexual stimulations and other means of temptation do
when you can hear your Lord calling you, saying:

﴿وَلَا تَقْرَبُواْ ٱلزِّنَىٰٓ إِنَّهُۥ كَانَ فَٰحِشَةً وَسَآءَ سَبِيلًا﴾

"And do not go near fornication. It is an abomination, and an evil way". [al-Isrā' 17:32]

He also says:

﴿وَقُل لِّلْمُؤْمِنَٰتِ يَغْضُضْنَ مِنْ أَبْصَٰرِهِنَّ وَيَحْفَظْنَ فُرُوجَهُنَّ﴾

"Say to the believing women that they should lower their eyes and guard their private parts". [an-Nūr 24:31]

He also says:

﴿قَدْ أَفْلَحَ ٱلْمُؤْمِنُونَ ۝ ٱلَّذِينَ هُمْ فِى صَلَاتِهِمْ خَٰشِعُونَ ۝ وَٱلَّذِينَ هُمْ عَنِ ٱللَّغْوِ مُعْرِضُونَ ۝ وَٱلَّذِينَ هُمْ لِلزَّكَوٰةِ فَٰعِلُونَ ۝ وَٱلَّذِينَ هُمْ لِفُرُوجِهِمْ حَٰفِظُونَ﴾

"It is the believers who are successful: those who are humble in their prayer; those who turn away from worthless talk; those who pay the zakāt; those who guard their private parts..." [al-Mu'minūn 23:1-5]

There is no doubt that when the Religion has become complete and fully integrated within you, i.e. it is your faith, your desire, your fear, your exaltation, your love, it will grant you amazing ability to be patient and firm.

For the Religion to be your desire, you only have to contemplate for a moment His ﷻ words:

﴿كُلُواْ وَٱشْرَبُواْ هَنِيٓـًٔا بِمَآ أَسْلَفْتُمْ فِى ٱلْأَيَّامِ ٱلْخَالِيَةِ﴾

"Eat and drink with relish for what you did before in days gone by". [al-Ḥāqqah 69:24]

For the Religion to be your fear, you only have to take a quick glance at His ﷻ words:

﴿وَيَوْمَ يُعْرَضُ ٱلَّذِينَ كَفَرُواْ عَلَى ٱلنَّارِ أَذْهَبْتُمْ طَيِّبَٰتِكُمْ فِى حَيَاتِكُمُ ٱلدُّنْيَا وَٱسْتَمْتَعْتُم بِهَا فَٱلْيَوْمَ تُجْزَوْنَ عَذَابَ ٱلْهُونِ بِمَا كُنتُمْ تَسْتَكْبِرُونَ فِى ٱلْأَرْضِ بِغَيْرِ ٱلْحَقِّ وَبِمَا كُنتُمْ تَفْسُقُونَ﴾

"On the Day when those who disbelieved are exposed to the Fire: 'You dissipated the good things you had in your worldly life and enjoyed yourself in it. So today you are being repaid with the punishment of humiliation for being arrogant in the earth without any right and for being deviators". [al-Aḥqāf 46:20]

And think about how humbling it is when He ﷻ says:

﴿قُلْ إِن كُنتُمْ تُحِبُّونَ ٱللَّهَ فَٱتَّبِعُونِى يُحْبِبْكُمُ ٱللَّهُ وَيَغْفِرْ لَكُمْ ذُنُوبَكُمْ وَٱللَّهُ غَفُورٌ رَّحِيمٌ﴾

"Say: 'If you love Allah then follow me. Allah will love you and forgive you for your wrong actions. Allah is Ever-Forgiving, Most Merciful.'" [Āl 'Imrān 3:31]

Reflecting on just one of these verses will guarantee – if one's faith is sincere and the various aspects of the Religion are completed and integrated – that you are given extraordinary power that cannot be described.

My dear young brother, the man who is tested with loving wealth and gathering it, or a beautiful woman, or some worldly commodity, will – in order to attain the object of his desire – plunge into a fire of lasting punishment and unshakable difficulty, because the love in one's heart can overcome the pain in one's body and feelings. Because of the intensity of his attachment to the objective that he seeks, he overcomes all the obstacles that stand in his way. He humbles himself and forgets his honour and his pride, because he sees that all the formative elements of his personality are of no value and of no benefit if they do not realise for him the objective that he is striving for.

This is the state of someone who is tested with one of the delights and passions of this world, so what about someone whose heart is attached to its Creator and is overflowing with feelings of love, exaltation, and reverence? What about someone whose mind and intellect are filled with certainty that He alone brings about benefit and harm, and that He is the One who creates the secret of bliss in the heart of everyone who is blissful and wretchedness in the feelings of everyone who is wretched? This person's essence melts under the authority of His ﷻ words:

﴿فَفِرُّوٓاْ إِلَى ٱللَّهِ إِنِّى لَكُم مِّنْهُ نَذِيرٌ مُّبِينٌ﴾

"So flee to Allah. Truly I bring you a clear warning from Him". [adh-Dhāriyāt 51:50]

I was once travelling in a car with two young people. Each introduced himself to the other and then they started talking. One of them said – and he had explained that he was one of those Arabs who had migrated to the farthest ends of America for the sake of provision –

that he was doing some mechanical job and earning close to $900 a month, and had he known that cleaning up trash would have earned him one more dollar, he would not have hesitated to do it and would have done so happily!

Then he went on to say that Arab swagger had no meaning when it came to the goal that he had migrated for, and he had only migrated for the sake of the dollar!

I listened very carefully to what this young man was saying, and I saw therein an immense lesson for anyone who wants to take heed. Nothing he said could be refuted or debated!

Indeed, being attached to an objective overcomes all obstacles that stand in its way, however lofty or lowly that objective is.

And therefore the one who sits and complains about how rough the road is only doing so because, in reality, he is not attached to the objective.

To put it differently, the one who surrenders to sexual stimulations and other forms of temptations and uses the excuse that he tried to be patient, and to be extra patient, but could not bear it is skirting the truth. His real excuse is that he is not attached to arriving at Allah's ﷻ pleasure.

My young brother, your patience with the stimulations and temptations that you see all around you is not more difficult than the patience that this other young man had when it came to leaving his homeland and his family, suffering vagrancy and isolation, and then breaking his dignity and sacrificing his reputation.

The difference between the two of you, however, is the extent to which each of you is attached to an objective. His attachment to the dollar, for the sake of which he embarked upon such a venture, is stronger than your attachment to your Creator, whose rule you profess to adhere to.

Therefore, nourish this attachment in both your mind and your heart, and reflect on the fact you are in the grip of your Creator ﷻ, that your final destination is to stand before Him, and that you are His slave; you have no control over yourself or your existence before Him.

Nourish this attachment by constantly reflecting on this reality, and seek assistance therein from the remembrance of Allah, in the morning and in the evening. Dedicate yourself to glorifying Him and seeking His forgiveness on a regular basis. Then, remember that there is no Prophet or Messenger except that he suffered more trials and afflictions than you do:

$$﴿فَمَا وَهَنُواْ لِمَآ أَصَابَهُمْ فِى سَبِيلِ ٱللَّهِ وَمَا ضَعُفُواْ وَمَا ٱسْتَكَانُواْ﴾$$

"They did not give up in the face of what assailed them in the Way of Allah, nor did they weaken, nor did they yield". [Āl 'Imrān 3:146]

Throughout all of this, be certain that if you are patient and seek refuge in Allah, by supplicating to Him and imploring Him from the depths of your soul, He will extract for you means of happiness that will deliver you from any deviation or temptation. Your Lord ﷻ has made this pledge and His words are perfectly clear:

$$﴿وَمَن يَتَّقِ ٱللَّهَ يَجْعَل لَّهُۥ مَخْرَجًا ۝ وَيَرْزُقْهُ مِنْ حَيْثُ لَا يَحْتَسِبُ﴾$$

"Whoever has *taqwā* of Allah, He will give him a way out, and provide for him from where He does not expect". [at-Ṭalāq 65:2-3]

However, dear young person, Allah loves to hear your intimate conversation with Him, to hear you implore Him, and to see you achieve the loftiest ranks of slavehood to Him, so let your face be covered in dust while you prostrate at length. Let your supplications be combined with sobbing and weeping. Manifest your extreme weakness to Him and your humble state, which will invoke mercy and kindness. If you do that, Allah will put you on the right path, and cause you to ascend to the ranks of the truly sincere and the truly devout, and He will show you His Clear Proof[35] just as He showed Yūsuf ﷺ before.[36]

As for the problems in homes, most of them are because of the contradictions that arise between the young Muslim and his family if they are negligent or antagonistic towards the Religion. I see no way to solve these problems other than to be wise, to be gentle, and to refrain from violence regardless of how bad the circumstances may be or become.

Talking about this problem and how to solve it reminds me of the policy of non-violence that Gandhi was known for in his various political works and efforts. There is no doubt that a large part of his success goes back to this policy of non-violence. If he had crowned this policy with true faith in Allah and His Messenger, he would have achieved an even greater success, above and beyond the world that he was in, and India today would be something else. However, he was not guided to such and that success was short-lived. Then everything went back, more or less, to the way it had been.[37]

---

35 Ar. *burhān*.
36 See Sūrat Yūsuf 12:24.
37 Read the book *The Story of My Experiments with Truth* by Mahatma Gandhi, for it contains some chapters that a Muslim can benefit from.

The young Muslim must make use of this policy of non-violence as an important, comprehensive starting point for Islamic morals and manners, and an inseparable part of Islam's overall structure. It is a policy that is beautifully embodied in His ﷻ words:

$$﴿وَلَا تَسْتَوِى ٱلْحَسَنَةُ وَلَا ٱلسَّيِّئَةُ ۚ ٱدْفَعْ بِٱلَّتِى هِىَ أَحْسَنُ فَإِذَا ٱلَّذِى$$

$$بَيْنَكَ وَبَيْنَهُۥ عَدَاوَةٌ كَأَنَّهُۥ وَلِىٌّ حَمِيمٌ﴾$$

"A good action and a bad action are not the same. Repel the bad with something better and, if there is enmity between you and someone else, he will be like a bosom friend". [Fuṣṣilat 41:34]

Many young people, however, are unaware of this reality, and they deal with their domestic problems in ways that only make them more severe and complicated. One of them will regard himself as a foreign element inside his own home, and will then treat his family accordingly. The only time he sees them is when he passes them in the hallway on the way to his room, after which he goes inside and locks himself in. He might sit down and eat with them, but only if he feels strongly compelled to do so. He spends the rest of his time away from them, barely partaking with them in anything, be it a special occasion, a celebration, a family meeting, or whatever else.

You need to know, my dear young brother, that such conduct is completely wrong.

By conducting yourself in this way, you are instilling in their hearts more reasons for them to be antagonistic towards you and to dislike the Religion.

As for their being antagonistic towards you, this is because it is normal for them to respond to your harshness with their own harshness, if they do not take things further such that a response would be necessary. **As for their dislike of the Religion,** it is because they consider your harshness to be part of your religiosity, and they will thus confirm for themselves that religiosity is connected to having a harsh personality, treating others harshly, and living an introverted life.

It is clear that not only are you mistaken in this behaviour but you are also preventing your family from having a clear picture of the True Religion. You are not calling them to Islam as Islam requires, which is to have exalted character in your conduct and how you treat them.

You should know that from the moment Allah ennobled you with the blessing of being upright upon His Religion, He made you responsible for calling others to this blessing with every means at your disposal.

You should know that in their stance regarding hearing the word of truth, people fall into two camps. There is one camp that will subject itself to research, debate, and knowledge, regardless of who they are researching and debating with. With these people, you need to use education, guidance, and sincere advice. **The other camp,** due to its own circumstances and reasons, will reject your education, your sincere advice, and your guidance. This is because it sees itself as having a higher station than you, or maybe some individuals among them enjoy certain qualities, such as those of a teacher or a leader.

The only way to deal with these people – especially in the beginning – is to show them (in your conduct and how you treat them) the perfect, exalted model of a young Muslim. When calling this camp to Islam, **it will suffice you to remain silent and let your exalted Islamic character call and speak on your behalf.**

It is clear that the two parents, regarding their young adult child, are of the second camp. You cannot guide them to the path of truth by being arrogant and haughty towards them, or by withdrawing from them and casting what is called scolding glances at their behaviour, no matter how much all of that is combined with admonition, sincere advice, and guidance.

Instead of the aforementioned, it would be better for you to multiply your goodness[38] towards them and to show them, through your conduct, that the Religion in your life has only increased you in loving them, striving to serve them, and dedicating yourself to pleasing them.

Instead of withdrawing from the family and isolating yourself when you are at home, it would be better for you **to make yourself a servant for the old and the young therein**. Give them whatever you can of yourself, your effort, your time, and your wealth, and make each of them feel very strongly that you love them and have their best interests at heart.

However parents may be and however their child may be, what parents really want from their child is to be shown more *birr* and to be given more help and assistance.

So, make this desire of theirs the starting point of solving your problems with them, the starting point of your calling to the truth that Allah the Exalted has ennobled you with, and you will find in their being pleased with your *birr* a strong cause for their being pleased with your religiosity and probity.

And you should not understand from what I am saying that you may turn a blind eye to those of Allah the Exalted's rulings that your parents dislike in order to show them *birr*, or that you must – instead of isolating yourself from the family – be present when one of them engages in sin or sit with them when they are doing something reprehensible.

---

38 Ar. *birr*, i.e. kindness, respect, and so forth.

No. I am not saying anything of the sort. **Rather, you should know that there is no obedience to a creation in disobedience to the Creator.**

However, what you must pay special attention to is your accurate application of Allah the Exalted's words:

﴿وَإِن جَٰهَدَاكَ عَلَىٰٓ أَن تُشْرِكَ بِى مَا لَيْسَ لَكَ بِهِۦ عِلْمٌ فَلَا تُطِعْهُمَا وَصَاحِبْهُمَا فِى ٱلدُّنْيَا مَعْرُوفًا﴾

"But if they try to make you associate something with Me about which you have no knowledge, do not obey them. Keep company with them correctly and courteously in this world". [Luqmān 31:15]

To clarify this, your father might forbid you from certain actions of worship, whether supererogatory or obligatory, **so what should your stance be?**

There is no doubt that Allah's command takes precedence over your father's command, and that disregarding his prohibition will not be considered recalcitrance[39] at all. However, recalcitrance could arise from *how* you disregard his prohibition.

What is required of you in this situation is to excuse yourself as gently and as peaceably as possible and then immerse this excusing of yourself with more *birr* towards him, more care and consideration for him, and more dedication to serving him. **You will find that this second treatment offers the best solution to the first problem.**

Nevertheless, there may be some parents who are excessive in their hatred of Islam, so much so that they will sacrifice their personal and

---

39 Ar. *'uqūq*.

psychological needs. The problem with them will not be solved by any treatment or attempting anything we have discussed. I do not think that their Muslim children have any way to solve the problem apart from patiently bearing with the same treatment.

A child's *birr* towards his parents is the best way to move whatever feelings are hidden in the deepest depths of their hearts. If the situation has reached the point where their hearts are devoid of all human values and feelings, persisting with *birr* and mercy is the best way to bring these feelings into existence.

If they do not come into existence, it suffices the child that through his efforts he has achieved a vast treasure of Allah's ﷻ pleasure, and if Allah is pleased with him, how can his parents' displeasure with him, despite his *birr*, harm him?

At this juncture, however, **I would like to address my final word to the parents**.

It is clear that I am not addressing any parent who rejects Islam and denies its doctrines and rulings, as there is no way for us to come together and understand one another.

Rather, I am addressing those parents who claim that they are Muslims, and maybe they attend the Friday prayer and some of the daily congregational prayers. Maybe you have seen them at some religious gatherings, adorning themselves with outward signs of Islam and using Islamic phrases and expressions.

They cannot stand it, however, when their children are religious and adorn themselves with sound Islamic awareness. They go to war with their children in every way possible, and use all manner of astonishing means to coerce their children into temptation and deviation. Maybe the taste of sin will carry them away and the pleasure of deviation will intoxicate them.

I know virtuous young people who have committed themselves to waking up in the pre-dawn hours so they can humbly stand before their Lord and beseech Him, but their parents, who are in the same house, see this as an unforgivable crime, or a type of insanity that is cause for concern. In fighting them and plotting against them, they sink to the lowest of levels, maybe lower than you can even imagine.

I know young Muslim women in whose hearts faith in Allah has become firmly embedded and thus they have answered Allah's command to protect themselves and cover. They have started drawing their outer garments closely around themselves,[40] but the fathers and mothers have become angered and enraged at this heedful answer to Allah's call and have combined their efforts to fight them, exasperate them, and conspire against them. Some of them have even gone as far as to restrict expenditure and livelihood. They are abundantly generous to the daughter who is wanton and far removed from the Religion while at the same time they stay away from her righteous sister, who is obeying her Lord's command and answering the call of her Religion, and show her anger and contempt.

To these parents I say my final word in this section:

As for Shayṭān's having achieved something, and getting what he wants from you, by causing you to follow certain paths of sin and disobedience, that is a personal matter and we have nothing to say about it,

---

40   (tn): See Sūrat al-Aḥzāb 33:59.

as there is nobody – after the Prophets – who is free from disobedience and sin. Rather, everyone makes mistakes, and the best of those who make mistakes are those who constantly repent.

However, it is very dangerous for an occurrence of disobedience in your life to turn into a path that you defend, a principle that you call to, and a truth that you guard and are extremely vigilant over. Disobedience – according to the creed of every Muslim – is a mistake that is made, unwillingly, and if the heart is not pained by it and made regretful, it does not make sense, under any circumstance, for the person to make it a banner that he calls to, that he defends, and for which he will fight the people closest to him!

You have been given something amazing, without being asked to do anything or to expend any effort, if Allah has blessed you with children whose tender hearts are overflowing with faith in Him, with love for Him, and with fear of Him. They are travelling the path of slavehood to Him ﷻ and they are adhering to the way that has been outlined by Allah's Messenger ﷺ and which he followed. This is because there is no righteous action by which they draw nearer to Allah ﷻ except that the same action is written on your scroll of deeds, and you will see its reward at a time when you are most in need of a tiny portion of it.

Yes, the righteous child, whether male or female, is a treasure that Allah bestows on his parents without any effort, and He makes his righteous life an extension of their lives. He makes his scroll of pure deeds an extension of each of their scrolls. When this world has come to an end, along with all the blessings and hardships it contains, and mankind is standing before the Lord of all Creation, this righteous child will be a barrier between his parents and the Fire, and his righteousness will be an expiation for their sins!

The Messenger of Allah ﷺ says in an agreed upon ḥadīth: {When the child of Adam dies, his deeds come to an end apart from three: on-going charity, knowledge that is benefitted from, and a righteous child who supplicates for him.}

And he says in another agreed upon ḥadīth: {Whoever is in charge[41] of daughters and is good to them, they will be a barrier between him and the Fire.}

Thus, what mistake could be greater than your looking at this immense blessing that Allah has bestowed upon you, without any effort on your part, and then trampling on it. Then, on top of that, you exert effort in order to turn it into another burden of sin that you, without any reason, will have to carry on your backs?

What harshness is worse than your looking at these pure young people, who have preferred, out of their desire to please Allah, to cling to uprightness and firmness upon the truth as if it were hot coal in their hands, patiently bearing with whatever trials come their way, and then you add to their torment by going to war with them, by being harsh with them, and doing everything you can to coerce them into sin and misguidance?

What kind of blind intrigue have you perpetrated? You claim to be Muslims but you would prefer for your children to be a barrier between you and the Paradise after Allah the Exalted has blessed you and made them a barrier between you and the Fire?

---

41 (tn): The Arabic word in this narration is *yalī*. In another narration, the word is *ubtu-liya*, i.e. tested. Imam an-Nawawī says in his commentary on *Ṣaḥīḥ Muslim*, 'He e called it a trial (*ibtilā'*) because people tend to dislike having daughters. Allah the Exalted has said: ﴿وَإِذَا بُشِّرَ أَحَدُهُم بِٱلْأُنثَىٰ ظَلَّ وَجْهُهُۥ مُسْوَدًّا وَهُوَ كَظِيمٌ﴾ "**When one of them is given the good news of a baby girl, his face darkens and he is furious.**" [an-Naḥl 16:58]' *Al-Minhāj fī Sharḥ Ṣaḥīḥ Muslim bin al-Ḥajjāj* (Riyadh: International Ideas Home, n.d.), 1562.

Leave them alone. Let them, whether they are male or female, free themselves so that they can focus on their Hereafter instead of their worldly lives. Let them have their pre-dawn hours, in which Allah has blessed them with intimate conversation and prostration to Him. Leave them to the Truth, which they believe in and love passionately, which is a creed in their hearts and conduct in their daily lives, or it is covering and modesty in their appearance and clothing. However, they have to be kinder to you than you are to yourselves, and exhaust their abilities and their strength to serve you, as long as you do not make them do something unlawful or coerce them into injustice and deviation.

Instead of fighting them, would it not be better for you to carry on sleeping and let the reward for their night prayers and their seeking forgiveness be written for you? Would it not be better to do no more than enjoy the delights and pleasures of this world while getting the reward for their abstention from and avoidance of the same? Would it not be better to do no more than indulge in sins and unlawful matters and let their seeking forgiveness and repentance on your behalf erase those sins?

Dear parents, exert yourselves so that your children grow up following the path of truth, and if you do not do that, do not make them follow the path of misguidance and sin. Help them stick to the path that leads to Allah's pleasure by being pleased with them, or at least remain silent.

If not, then after you, there is no enemy, or colonisation, or orientalism who opposes the Truth and the Religion. After the misguidance and error that you are perpetrating, there is no overwhelming trial or devastating test that Muslims can be exposed to. Among all of your deeds you will not find any that will cause more regret tomorrow than what you are doing now.

As for you, O youth, you must know that the result of everything we have mentioned by way of the various treatments for your problems **is nothing other than patience!** Be patient with everything that impedes you on the way to Allah, and seek help from Allah's ﷻ *tawfīq*.[42] If you do that, Allah will love you. If Allah loves you, you will love Him, and when you love Him, He will make every trial and anguish easy for you.

This is what you can refer to in Allah the Exalted's Book:

﴿وَأَصْبِرْ وَمَا صَبْرُكَ إِلَّا بِٱللَّهِ﴾

"Be patient, and your patience is only by Allah".
[an-Naḥl 16:127]

﴿وَٱللَّهُ يُحِبُّ ٱلصَّـٰبِرِينَ﴾

"Allah loves the steadfast". [Āl 'Imrān 3:146]

﴿وَبَشِّرِ ٱلْمُخْبِتِينَ ۝ ٱلَّذِينَ إِذَا ذُكِرَ ٱللَّهُ وَجِلَتْ قُلُوبُهُمْ وَٱلصَّـٰبِرِينَ عَلَىٰ مَآ أَصَابَهُمْ﴾

"Give good news to the humble-hearted, whose hearts tremble at the mention of Allah and who are steadfast in the face of all that happens to them". [al-Ḥajj 22:34-35]

I ask Allah to place all of us under the authority of these verses and to seal our lives upon righteous deeds, and all praise is for Allah, Lord of all Creation.

---

42 (tn): i.e. His enabling success.

Printed in Great Britain
by Amazon